Marriage and Family Enrichment Bible Studies

Sunday T. Eke-Okoro, Dr.Med.Sc., M.Sc., M.Div.

All Scripture quotations, unless otherwise indicated are taken from The Holy Bible New International Version, Zondervan Bible Publishers, Grand Rapids, Michigan.

Copyright © 2005 Sunday T. Eke-Okoro, Dr.Med.Sc., M.Sc., M.Div

All rights reserved. No part of this publication may be reproduced, stored in a retrieval system, or transmitted in any form or by any means, electronic, mechanical, photocopying, recording, or otherwise, without the prior written permission of the publisher.

ISBN: 0-9769957-9-4

Published by:
Holy Fire Publishing
531 Constitution Blvd. Martinsburg, WV 25401
www.ChristianPublish.com

Printed in the United States of America and the United Kingdom

Table of Contents

Dedication	5
Preface	7
Introduction	9
Study One: Matrimonial and Familial Love Expression.....	19
Study Two: Divine Principle of Love	23
Study Three: Sustenance of Matrimonial Love	29
Study Four: Trinitarian Structure of Marriage	35
Study Five: Searching for a Suitable Spouse	45
Study Six: Jew-Gentile Factor in Marriage	51
Study Seven: Procreation in Marriage	57
Study Eight: Socialization of Children	65
Study Nine: An Exploration of Peace in Marriage and Family	71
Study Ten: Family as a Functional Unit	77
Study Eleven: Restoration of Cordial Relations	83
Study Twelve: Effects of Mortality on Marriage and Family	89
Study Thirteen: Divorce	95
Study Fourteen: Illumination of Spousal Equality	101
Study Fifteen: The Family Altar	109
Study Sixteen: Chauvinistic Tendencies	115
Study Seventeen: Keeping the Faith	125

Study Eighteen: Role of a Father 131
Study Nineteen: Role of Mother 137
Study Twenty: Factors in Marriage and Family 143

Dedication

To the Trinitarian Structure of Marriage in which God is Part of the Union of Husband and Wife.

Preface

This book is an attempt to put together the teachings of the Holy Scriptures on marriage and family for Bible studies. No single chapter of the Bible contains an aggregate of materials that can inform on the various areas of biblical teaching on marriage and family. The result is that Bible studies on Marriage and Family are rare in many congregations. Marriage and Family are under serious satanic attack. The more we do Bible studies in this area, the more people are aware of the tricks of the devil and would be better armed to confront the enemy. Marriages need to endure in peace and harmony and the same should be the case for the family. There is the need to talk about the problem of instability and breakdown of these important relations that determine the worth of humans. The light of Jesus should be made to fall on our marriages and families through the enrichment derived from Bible studies.

These Bible studies would stimulate spouses to open up and lay everything on the table for divine intervention. The twenty studies in this book could not be said to contain all that can be discussed, but they are a very helpful guide. Their utilization will help in an illumination of the various aspects of marriage and family through the mediation of the Holy Spirit. It is believed that these studies will, by the grace of God, contribute to a better understanding of marriage and family issues, thereby provide insight into ways of restoring peace, harmony and endurance in relationships.

Married and unmarried persons will benefit from these studies. Churches, families, marriage counselors and seminary students will find this book a helpful resource. The companion book is, *Family Love and Spousal Equity*. All glory and honor to God the Father, God the Son, and God the Holy Spirit who has made this book a great possibility. My thanks also go to Sister Patricia Ezike who read the manuscript and made helpful suggestions.

Sunday T. Eke-Okoro

Introduction

Marriage is not a bed of roses but a ministry field in which you will need to make commitments, sacrifices and invest your talent to make it work. People come to Church wearing masks on their faces. After worship the masks are removed at home and they begin to face the realities of life as they are encumbered with the problems of broken marriages and families. Many of us are still unaware that the enemy of marriage and family is the devil. Spouses are in the business of pointing accusing fingers on one another instead of bracing themselves for battle against the goliath of our marriages and families. Every family needs a David to stand up against the goliath in the name of our Mighty God of heaven and earth. There is the need to talk about the problem of instability and breakdown of these important relations that determine the worth of humans. The light of Jesus should be made to fall on our marriages and families through the enrichment derived from Bible studies. Churches and other religious organizations should recognize the need for more frequent Bible studies on marriage and family.

Destroyer of Marriage and Family
The most helpful means of interpreting the disruptions that occur in our lives is through a biblical statement in which Jesus said that the thief comes only to steal, kill and destroy. In contrast, Jesus said that

he himself came that we may have life, and have it in full. The thief in Jesus' statement refers to Satan. Therefore, Satan comes only to steal, kill and destroy. The ultimate aim of Satan is to cause destruction. Sin is a destroyer employed by Satan. We are all children of God. Satan is not happy that we belong to God. He wants to steal us from God. Therefore he employs various wicked means to take us away from God. When he successfully lures a person from God, he may use that one as his agent by making that person live a life of sin. He who does what is sinful is of the devil, because the devil has been sinning from the beginning. The reason why Jesus came was to destroy the works of the devil. Because Jesus lives in us, we cannot continue in the practice of sin.

When God created humankind and placed them in the beautiful Garden of Eden, the man and the woman enjoyed cordiality and harmony in relationship between both of them and with God. Satan was not happy with the excellent relations in the Garden of Eden. He planned a disruption by employing a destroyer called sin, which attacked the woman Eve. The man and his wife lost the favor of the Lord and were driven away from the beautiful Garden of Eden. Satan's attack on the people who lived in the Garden of Eden changed God's plan for his creation. The mess which Satan caused at the Garden of Eden has continued to be the basis of present-day problems of humanity.

Identify of the Enemy

Satan who is also known as the devil is still on the loose, prowling around like a roaring lion looking for someone to devour. We are advised to be self-controlled and alert in firmness of faith as we resist him. Satan goes about all over the world causing suffering on people. It is disturbing that many people do not yet understand that their problems are caused by the devil. They continue to blame one another because they are unaware of the devices of the devil. Your problem is caused by the devil, but God knows about it and Jesus is able to deliver you from the mess of the devil.

The people of God are in the warfront fighting Satan. Satan joined a group of angels who came to present themselves to God. He thought he could successfully hide himself, but to his surprise God detected him. God asked him where he came from. Satan replied, "From roaming through the earth and going back and forth in it."[1] Therefore, be careful and watch out for attacks from Satan, your wicked enemy. He prowls around like a roaring lion looking for someone to devour.[2] Therefore prepare your mind for action; think clearly and exercise self-control. It is when you lack self-control that your enemy, the devil can have a foothold in you to cause destruction. All you need to do is to submit yourself to God in holiness. "Resist the devil and he will flee from you."[3]

---

[1] Job 1:7, Job 2:2
[2] 1 Peter 5:8
[3] James 4:7

It is a struggle which many do not conceive and are hardly prepared for. It is not a struggle between you and your spouse, but against evil forces driven by Satan. The ultimate aim of this evil force is to trip you off in order to steal you, kill you and destroy you. Therefore, be strong in the Lord and in his mighty power, fully armed with the whole armor of God, so that when Satan and his agents come on you, you will be able to stand your ground and win a great victory.[4]

Self-control

The most important single attitude, which can make you play into the hand of the devil is when you fail to exercise self-control. In marital sexual activity, spouses should not deprive each other except by mutual consent and for a time, so that they may devote themselves to prayer. "Then come together again so that Satan will not tempt you because of your lack of self-control."[5] If spouses deprive each other, they could give Satan room to manipulate the mind for extramarital sexual immorality. One way to "flee from sexual immorality"[6] is for spouses not to deprive each other. We all therefore need to be self-controlled, putting on faith and love as a breastplate, and the hope of salvation as a helmet.[7] It is not only in relation to sexual immorality,

---

[4] Ephesians 6:10-18
[5] 1 Corinthians 7:5
[6] 1corinthians 6:18
[7] 1 Thessalonians 5:8

but also to protect us from satanic manipulation to commit other sins. It is a state of war. Satan is determined trip us off our faith in order to steal, kill and destroy. Self-control is derived from fixing our eyes on Jesus, the author and perfecter of our faith, from beginning to the end.[8]

Bible Studies are Invaluable

Marriage and family should always be discussed to help people deal with what they are silently passing through. When people open up and release the burden of their hearts during Bible studies, they are able to share experiences, receive counsel from each other, and are thereby encouraged. Above all, the Holy Spirit is invited to take control and bring healing. The close relationship between the Church, marriage and family should be an important stimulus to give more time to deal with marriage and family issues. When family and marriage are good, the Church will be good, but when they are bad the situation will invariably reflect on the Church. The instability and other problems of marriage and family are before the throne of the Almighty requesting for a proper presentation and eventual healing.

God is part of the marital union of husband and wife. This defines its Trinitarian structure. Without God as part of the union, the marriage will not work. It will fail. God glues the spouses into

---

[8] Hebrews 12:1-2

one flesh with love. There is therefore the important need to present our marriage and family problems to God as soon as they surface, so as to obtain an immediate healing. When marriage problems are unduly prolonged, they result in disastrous consequences. They need to be dealt with as soon as they occur. An illumination of the spiritual nature of marriage and all its problems can be readily made possible through relevant Bible studies as hurting spouses prayerfully present their issues to God. God has given spouses love to target on each other. Spouses cannot imprison love and feel comfortable. Any attempt to imprison love within you would always be met with a stiff resistance. Love is always a winner. It would somehow find a way out and touch other lives. Love exists with peace.

Working on your Marriage

When you cannot express love, it implies that you are not a child of God, and therefore you do not have love. If you do not have love, you also do not have peace. Ignore the expression of love, and you will find yourself rejecting the peace you very much need. Therefore, if you do not need peace, go ahead and ignore the expression of love. Most marital and family problems derive from a refusal of people to touch others with sincere love. It is important to know that to increase inner peace, there should be an unmitigated expression of love. When a man and a woman come together for a marriage relationship they are primed in love for each other. The degree of love expression among them helps in a better understanding of their degree of compatibility.

Much of our marriage and family problems are connected to an improper choice of marriage partners. People need to do a better job in their search for a suitable spouse to avoid investing in trouble at home. God found the suitable wife for Adam and he is the one who is to find a suitable wife for you. The use of the word "suitable" indicates that there are many wives out there but only one is suitable for you. To get to that suitable wife, there is the important need to make an ordered search. One of the studies in this book describes three important areas of importance during the search for a suitable wife or husband.

You must know that you have to work on your marriage before it can succeed. There is no perfect person and there is no perfect marriage. You must be determined to work on your marriage and aim at perfection in the future. You and your marriage have to pass through fire before you can come forth as gold. We all carry baggages into marriage but we have to deal with each others faults with commonsense and with wisdom. Nothing should separate you from the love of God given to you by God himself at marriage. Hang in there, and refuse to submit to devil's trick to dislodge you from the matrimonial union, which God has sealed with his love. Never take away your love from your spouse because he/she has messed up. Help to prop him/her up and thereby provide the modalities for necessary healing to occur. It will eventually be all right and you will be in a good position to give testimonies of the goodness of the Lord. No cross, no crown is also true in marriage. You must not ignore God in your relationship.

Family and Socialization

Children born to a family help to strengthen the bonds of love and unity. Children help marriages to endure. A fruitful marriage is procreating and generally stronger than a non-procreating marriage. This does not mean that a non-procreating marriage does not have what it takes to endure. In fact, it has no reason to go apart if love has been well-established between the spouses, especially in the Trinitarian model. Socialization of children is not solely the duty of parents. The training of children involves the whole community, the whole nation, and special agencies. Parents may do an excellent job at home in giving sound biblical training to their children, but when they are sent out to other agents of socialization things go bad. The best training that parents give to their children is Bible-based. Other agents of socialization that do not draw upon biblical instructions fail to meet the goals of child training. It is very important to submit our public school system to God. Chaplains should be employed to guide moral education in our public schools.

We need to resist the devil there, and he will flee from our children. If we come near to God, he will come near to us.[9]

The family can be likened to the body of Christ in which there are many members working together as a unit. The family is a secure place of rest, care and protection. It is the center for salvation and redemption. It is a body of people bound together as a unit by love and called to a peaceful co-existence.

[Each of you in the family should look not only to your own interests, but also to the interest of other family members.]

---

[9] (James 4:7-10).

Study One

Topic: Matrimonial and Familial Love Expression

Text: During the first marriage in the Garden of Eden, Adam was pleased to have a suitable helper to receive his love. It must be mentioned that love is always pushing out its way through from inside of a person to the external environment to touch lives and make a difference. You cannot imprison love and feel comfortable. Any attempt to imprison love within you would always be met with a stiff resistance. Love is always a winner. It would somehow find a way out and touch other lives. Eve could not eat the forbidden fruit alone without giving some of it to her husband, Adam. Adam could not refuse the fruit because it was given to him as an act of love. Again he loved his wife and believed that she would always give her what was good. Although it turned out to be negative, it was not the original intent of the spouses. The problem was that their love did not target God first before targeting each other.

Spouses produce lasting influence on each other only through acts of love. Love generates faithfulness and trust. "He who pursues righteousness and love finds life, prosperity and honor."[10] A marriage adopts a specific characteristic that is dependent on how spouses express love for each other. In fact, everything for which a family is known originates from their pattern of love expression.

This is because the quality of a relationship is a function of the degree of love expression in that relationship. Since love is from God, spouses will need to be firmly connected to God to ensure the sustenance of sincere love in their relationship. The special features of love can only be seen in spousal relationship if God continues to be part of the marriage relationship. Divine love is patient and kind. It neither boasts nor manifests pride. It is not rude, not selfish, not easily angered, does not keep record of wrongs, and does not enjoy evil practices. Divine love has nothing to do with lies, but it rejoices with the truth.[11] In marriage and other family relationships, love provides protection, always hopes, trusts, and perseveres. There is much sense in this because in marriage and family, people seek care and protection, which can only be provided in love.

When family love first targets God, there will be peace in the home; marriage and family will also be flourishing and enduring. When a person does not touch other people with the love God has given that one for outward expression, that person experiences war within and without as peace is taken away. In the habitat of love, there is peace and harmony. Love exists with peace. When you cannot express love, it implies that you are not a child of God, and therefore you do not have love. If you do not have love, you also do not have peace. Ignore the expression of love, and you will find

---

[10] (Proverbs 21:21)
[11] (1 Corinthians 13)

yourself rejecting the peace you very much need. Therefore, if you do not need peace, go ahead and ignore the expression of love.

When people accuse you of not having love for other people, they are not saying that your bank of love is emptied of love. People are only referring to your refusal to draw upon the love God has put in you to touch other lives. If you do not love, then you hate and if you hate, you deny yourself of peace. Hate may result in disastrous consequences, which you did not bargain for. God has commanded us to imitate him as his beloved children and live a life of love because God is love and Christ the beloved Son of God loved us and gave his life for our redemption.[12] We love because God our Father loved us first by his exemplary love revealed when he gave his beloved Son Jesus Christ to die for our sake. For the Son of God to agree to die for wretched sinners is an unprecedented demonstration of love. This shows that love must not be selfish. Of course, if your action is selfish, it could not be a demonstration of love. Apostle Paul said that we should make every effort to do what leads to peace and mutual edification. The only thing that we can do that would lead to peace and mutual edification is an act of love.[13]

[Each of you in the family should look not only to your own interests, but also to the interest of other family members.]

---

[12] (Ephesians 5:1-2)
[13] (Romans 14:19)

Quest

1. What are the consequences of love imprisonment or non-expression of love?
2. Why did Eve give the forbidden fruit to her husband, and why did her husband take it from her without asking questions?
3. What determines the descriptors of a marriage or a family?
4. Why are people of God advised to imitate God and live a life of love? (Ephesians 5:1-2).
5. How can spouses produce lasting influence on each other?
6. Is there any person who is incapable of expressing love?
7. What must be done to guarantee the sustenance of marital and family love?
8. Are there people who can be said to be unlovable? Give reasons to support your answer.
9. What are the main traits of sincere love in marriage and family?
10. Explain the state of the bank of love of a person who does not express love.

Memory Verse: Love is patient, love is kind. It does not envy, it does not boast, it is not proud.[14]

---

[14] 1 Corinthians 13:4

Study Two

Topic: Divine Principle of Love

Text: Love is an outward expression of the nature of God. Marriage and family are born and nurtured in love. God is love and to love is to be of God. Love is sincere, holy and divine. Love must not be misplaced for ulterior motives since it has no role in evil. Love has got to be love. God is love that creates, nurtures, beautifies and generates peace. In the beginning, God desired to have a target for divine love. He created humankind in his image to be a target for his love. He also filled humankind with divine love that needs expression outside of the person. Biblical injunction is that we should love one another for love comes from God. Love is divine. Everyone who loves is born of God and knows God. The person who does not love does not know God, because God is love.[15]

God found in Adam a target for divine love. He lavished his love on Adam, placing him in the beautiful Garden of Eden that approximated the beauty of heaven. God created beasts of the field and birds of the air and asked Adam to name them. Those animals and birds had companions, but Adam had none. "But for Adam, no suitable helper was found."[16] This citation informs that there were helpers, but there was no suitable helper for Adam. God filled Adam with divine love, but he had no human target for his love. He needed

---

[15] (1 John 4:7-8)

a suitable helper to target his God-given love. The type of love God gave to Adam was divine love that was not selfish. Adam therefore needed a human target for his love. God showed his love for Adam when he noted that "It is not good for the man to be alone. I will make a helper suitable for him."[17] God therefore caused Adam to fall into deep sleep during which he took one of his ribs. God made a woman from the rib he took out from the body of Adam. The woman became the suitable helper for Adam. In appreciation of the goodness of the Lord, Adam said about his suitable helper, "This is now bone of my bones and flesh of my flesh; she shall be called woman for she was taken out of man."[18]

The suitable helper of Adam was the woman named Eve. She became the wife of Adam and the target of his love. The woman Eve was also filled with divine love that targeted her husband. It can be seen that love is given to us for expression. Love must come out of each of us to touch other people's lives. Since love is given to us for expression, it is always struggling to come out of a person to make people feel good. However, if love is not allowed to come out and touch lives, it would continue to fight its way through a person. During such struggles, there is a loss of inner peace in a person who obstructs the way of love. You need to free the love in you in order to enjoy an inner peace. If you prefer to express hate instead of love,

---

[16] (Gen 2:20)
[17] (Gen 2:18)
[18] (Gen 2.23)

there will be war within and outside of your person. People will not like to associate with you because you have imprisoned love which they need. You will suffer Adamic loneliness without a suitable helper.

It will be noted that since Eve was a product of love, she was filled with love that needed expression outside of her. The target of her love was her husband. The reciprocal love seen in the mutual relationship between Adam and Eve at marriage could not exhaust their inborn love. They needed more targets for their love. It must be known that love is inexhaustible. The more you express love, the more God gives you love to express. The inventory of love is stocked pilled by God. If we have love for one another, we are recognized as children of God. God loves us and wants us to continue to be his children. He therefore characterizes us with love, which is his own nature. God showed his love for us when he sent his only Son Jesus Christ into the world to die for our sins that we may live through him. "This is love: not that we loved God, but that he loved us and sent his Son as an atoning sacrifice for our sins. Dear friends, since God so loved us, we also ought to love one another."[19] Our love firstly goes back to God who has given it to us, then secondly to people around us. Training in the expression of love begins in the family and the internship is generally done also in the family.

---

[19] (1 John 4:11-11)

In the community of heaven, life is lived in relationship. Relationship is only possible if it is based on love. When God created humankind, he decided that we should live and work in relationship. Since worthwhile relationship is only possible in love, God poured out his love on us that we may have love for him and for one another. We love because God first loved us. If anyone says that he/she loves God but yet hates his brother/sister, he is a liar. If you cannot love your brother/sister, whom you see, it means that you cannot love God, whom you cannot see with your physical eyes. Whoever loves God must also love his brother and sister.[20]

[Each of you in the family should look not only to your own interests, but also to the interest of other family members.]

Quest
1. Define love.
2. What are the characteristics of love? (1 Corinthians 13).
3. In what ways did God show his love for Adam?
4. Discuss the implications of the following statement, "But for Adam, no suitable helper was found." (Gen 2:20b).
5. What are the dangers of a lack of love expression?
6. In what ways may love be used for ulterior motives?
7. Explain your understanding of the principle of love?

---
[20] (1 John 4:19-21)

8. Why do you consider it necessary that love should be part of any meaningful relationship?
9. Your spouse calls you from his/her office to share an experience at the place of work. You ignore him/her or you do not give sufficient telephone time for discussion. What could be the dangers posed by your attitude?
10. Can you love God when you do not love your neighbor?
11. How should love be applied when looking for a life partner?

Memory Verse: We know and rely on the love God has for us. God is love. Whoever lives in love lives in God, and God in him.[21]

---

[21] (1 John 4:16)

Study Three

Topic: Sustenance of Matrimonial Love

Text: The understanding that God is love means that the ordering of love must be consistent with biblical precepts. The checks and balances in the expression of love should be well ordered in marriage and family relationships. It is basic to know that to increase inner peace, there should be an unmitigated expression of love. When a man and a woman come together for a marriage relationship they are primed in love for each other. The degree of love expression between them helps in a better understanding of their degree of compatibility. A very high degree of compatibility, which of course derives from sincere love for one another, would indicate that both of them should be able to live together in peace and harmony and the marriage would endure.

It is well known that some dating love have not been sincere but pretend to be so. The woman or the man may secretly be having a second person in life. Love in such a case could not be sincere despite dramatized kissing and lavish expenditure of resources. Love expression in dating must address the fact that a man cannot serve two masters. You should not deceive your partner during dating. This is a serious business in which you wish to determine the suitability of your dating partner for marriage. If you are already dating somebody for marriage, why not be done with that person before going in for another person. This is why dating partners should avoid sexual knowledge of partner during dating. Some go in for dating to mess you up, while at the back of their mind they have settled on who they want to marry. It is also known that one partner may be seriously searching for a marriage partner, while the other partner's only objective is to have sex. This is a deceptive use of love. In fact, it is no love because love does not delight in evil.

The foundation of marriage is love. This love is divine, and divine love is a sincere love. If love becomes weak, the marriage will be weakened and may eventually disintegrate. However, divine matrimonial love is usually sincere and quite strong to support marriage. Marriages that do not endure have not been established on love. In order to obtain divine matrimonial love, your marriage partner must come through divine approval. Marriage is a serious contract in which God who is love must have a principal role. Both a good wife and a good husband are gifts from God. In order to receive this gift, you must first seek the counsel of the Lord. The counsel of the Lord must be confirmed by the counsel of the people of God. These counsels must be reflected in the outpouring of sincere reciprocal love of prospective spouses on each other. This is your first love for one another and it is a gift from God. God gave you this love because he has approved your marriage. It is here suggested that prospective spouses should also undergo a medical examination to ensure that there is no dangerous health condition that could have a negative effect on the marriage.

When marriage has occurred, spouses are duty-bound to sustain their first love. First love must not be forgotten. It must be strengthened from time to time through redating of your spouse. Redating makes it possible for you to continue to remember your first love and be able to sustain it through life. If you forget your first love, you are certainly going to stray away from your marriage vows.[22] The danger is a destabilization of marriage bonds and an eventual collapse of the union. If you have any encouragement from being united with Christ in your marriage, comfort from his love, fellowship with the Spirit, tenderness and compassion, then make the joy of the Lord complete by being like-minded, having the same love, being one in spirit and purpose. Do nothing out of selfish ambition or vain conceit, but in humility consider your spouse and other members of your family better than yourself. Each of you should look not only to your own interests but also to the interest of your spouse and other members of your family.[23]

Matrimonial expression of love is reflected in mutual respect of spouses for each other. Spouses are to mutually submit to one another out of reverence for Christ.[24] You feel good doing this because you are one flesh with your spouse. What you do for your

---

[22] (Revelation 2:4-5)
[23] (Philippians 2:1-4)
[24] (Ephesians 5:21, 33)

spouse is what you do for yourself. There is no difference. There should be no separation of the union. Spouses should know that the mystery of their union is that it is symbolic of the body of Christ, which is the Church. "For this reason a man will leave his father and mother and be united to his wife, and the two will become one flesh."[25] Love is the basis of unity of married couples. Husband and wife become one flesh at marriage as they function in the context of Trinitarian unity. Trinitarian unity of couples ensures that God is part of your marriage relationship.

Mutuality in action is strengthened through self-differentiation. Each self-differentiated spouse is a person who is not cunning but says what he/she wishes to say and does what he/she wishes to do. You need to be a person of your own words. Love is perfect. It has nothing to do with lies and deception. Spouses must work in the trustworthiness of personal integrity. "The integrity of the upright guides them, but the unfaithful are destroyed by their duplicity."[26] The faithfulness of God defines his love and your faithfulness should also define your love for your spouse. Everything God does is based on love. When you see the works of God you see the results of divine expression of love. The works of God are reflections of his acts of love. If your marriage is an act of God, then it should reflect love in all its ramifications. Your marriage must be

---

[25] (Ephesians 5:31-32)
[26] (Proverbs 11:3)

surrounded by love. Spouses must always be there for each other no matter what. Spouses come into marriage, not as perfect individuals. They all come with their baggages that are at variance with those of the partner. However, love helps them to compassionately work on their baggages for improvement without disrupting their marriage relationship.

[Each of you in the family should look not only to your own interests, but also to the interest of other family members.]

Quest

1. How must love be expressed in order to derive personal peace?
2. What are the characteristics of sincere love? (1 Corinthians 13:4 - 7)
3. How may the expression of love determine the compatibility of a man and a woman for marriage?
4. Discuss insincerity of love expression during some dating process?
5. Suggest ways in which dating can circumvent exploitation of a partner?
6. Explain the mystery of marriage in relation to the body of Christ, which is the Church. (Ephesians 5:31-32).
7. Explain the concept of self-differentiation in marriage.

8. What baggages could spouses bring into a marriage? Suggest what should be spousal approach to these baggages.
9. Explain the three factors that should not be ignored during the selection of your spouse for marriage.
10. Do you think that a medical examination of prospective spouses is necessary before marriage?
11. How may Ephesians 5:21 be helpful in the sustenance of matrimonial love?
12. Discuss 1 Corinthians 7:1-11.

Memory Verse: Yet I have this against you: You have forsaken your first love. Remember the height from which you have fallen! Repent and do the things you did at first. If you do not repent, I will come to you and remove your lamp stand from its place.[27]

---

[27] (Revelation 2:4-5)

Study Four

Topic: Trinitarian Structure of Marriage

Text: The Triune union in which God is worshipped as God the Father, God the Son and God the Holy Spirit is the Trinity. God is part of the marital union of husband and wife. This defines its Trinitarian structure. Without God as part of the union, the marriage will not work. It will fail. God glues the spouses into one flesh with love. There is sense in this understanding because God is love. God has put the union together and what God has put together no one should separate. Jesus said, "Haven't you read that at the beginning the Creator made them male and female and said, for this reason a man will leave his father and mother and be united to his wife, and the two will become one flesh? So they are no longer two, but one. Therefore what God has joined together, let man not separate."[28] This is why marriage is a mystery. Two people from different families, and may be, from different geographical locations unite and become the best friends to each other. Apart from God, they are number one to each other. In fact, marriage is nothing short of a miracle.

When Jesus sent out his disciples ahead of him to every town and place where he was about to go, he sent them out in twos.[29] It was not good for a disciple to go alone; each disciple on mission

---

[28] (Matthew 19:4-6)

needs a suitable help-mate. It is interesting that two disciples go out with a single purpose to be fruitful and multiply and fill the earth with children of God. Though they were two persons, they function in unity like one person. "Do two walk together unless they have agreed to do so?"[30] The Trinitarian image is made obvious by the presence of Jesus with his disciples as they go out to proclaim the Gospel. "And surely I am with you always, to the very end of the age."[31] It is therefore not surprising that the disciples returned to report, "Lord, even the demons submit to us in your name."[32] Spouses are in ministry, sent out in twos to impact the world in very significant ways that should bring honor to God. Demons should submit to them and not vice versa.

The Trinitarian image of marriage makes it imperative that love should characterize the union. The presence of God in the union defines the presence of love in it. The man and the woman come together in love to be blessed by God who is the source of love. For matrimonial love to be sustained, God must always be part of the union. Divine assurance for the spouses in the Trinitarian union may be drawn from, "I will instruct you and teach you in the way you should go; I will counsel you and watch over you."[33] Provided spouses do not ignore God, the Lord's presence in their

---

[29] Luke 10:1
[30] Amos 3:3
[31] Matthew 28:20
[32] Luke 10:17

union is a guarantee that he would never leave nor forsake them. Faith in God is very important in the marital union. It is the only way spouses can please God and sustain the union with their first love. Satan does not like the connection of God in the marital union. Satan works very hard to destroy the love between the spouses in order to distance them from God and thereby destroy the Trinitarian nature of the marital union. After all, Satan has come to steal, kill and destroy. His first action is to sow seeds of discord between the spouses in an attempt to eliminate love. He may present fake alternatives that would distance them from God. When God is not in the union, love would also not be there and spouses could not operate harmoniously outside the domain of love. Do not let Satan have an inroad into your marriage. Yours is a holy matrimony that should not tolerate the mess of the devil. God is the guarantor of your marriage contract, not Satan who comes to destroy your peace, which matrimonial love generates.

There are various ways by which Satan may try to destroy your marriage. The most frequently used tool of the devil is infidelity. Satanic strategies in the use of infidelity are usually unexpected. Let us examine the following examples:

1. A man's wife persuaded her husband to allow her girlfriend to stay temporarily in their home. She had been ejected from her

---

[33] Psalm 32:8

apartment by her landlord. She moved in and developed a dangerous intimacy with her friend's husband. The man began extramarital affair with their guest. His wife began to notice some uncomfortable experiences that made her suspicious of the activities of her husband and her friend. She set up a trap by which she finally caught them in the very act of adultery. This act of infidelity ruined their marriage. "A man who commits adultery lacks judgment; whoever does so destroys himself."[34] They had shown hospitality to a homeless lady whom they did not know was an agent of the devil. At the conclusion of divorce, the man turned round and married the guest lady who Satan had used to destroy their good marriage. This does not mean that we should not show hospitality when the need arises. All we need to do is to first seek the counsel of the Lord before we do anything. It implies that prayers must not be ignored even when you want to do something good.

The Israelites during the reign of King David wanted to bring the Ark of God from Kiriath Jearim to Jerusalem, but ran into a very serious problem that caused them the life of Uzzah, who was among those guiding the movement of the Ark of God. They moved the Ark from Abinadab's house towards Jerusalem. Uzzah and his brother Ahio were guiding it during this journey.[35]

---

[34] (Proverbs 6:32)
[35] 2 Samuel 6:3

While David and the Israelites were celebrating during the journey of the Ark, the oxen stumbled and the Ark was about to fall to the ground. Uzzah reached out his hand to stop the Ark from falling. The anger of the Lord burned against Uzzah, and he died.[36] The problem was that, the Israelites did not inquire of the Lord on how to bring back the Ark. David later summoned the leaders of Levites and said to them, "You are the heads of the Levitical families; you and your fellow Levites are to consecrate yourselves and bring up the Ark of the Lord, the God of Israel, to the place I have prepared for it. It was because you, the Levites, did not bring it up the first time that the Lord our God broke out in anger against us. We did not inquire of him about how to do it in the prescribed way."[37]

It will be seen that it was a good thing to return the Ark of God to a home made for it by King David, but the method they adopted the first time was wrong. That was why it cost them the life of Uzzah. No matter the good you wish to do, you need to be prayerful in order to determine the will of God. You may also be doing the will of God with a wrong approach. You must first seek the counsel of God in everything, irrespective of whether you consider that what you are doing is right. The counsel of God is easy. All you need to do is to pray and tell God about

---

[36] (1 Chronicles 13:5-10)
[37] (1 Chronicles 15:11-13)

your plan before you set out to execute it. "Commit to the Lord whatever you do, and your plans will succeed."[38] Once you commit your actions to the hand of God, go ahead and do it because God is with you. The additional thing you must do as a spouse is to discuss your plans with your spouse and agree on what you will have to do. In fact, your discussion should be strongly connected to your prayerful presentation of the matter to God who is the Lord of your marriage and family.

2. Many marriages have been destroyed by the devil operating in work places. Some people go to their jobs and build immoral sexual relationships that predispose their marriage to destruction. Some bosses convert their junior workers who may be other people's wives or husbands into sexual partners at the workplace. Other immoral relationships that do not necessarily involve bosses occur in the workplace and these also destroy marriages. A spouse may stay long hours at work possibly doing overtime to make extra money for the family, while the ungrateful spouse at home connives with strange sexual partners to spend the money and also destroy the marriage as a result of adultery. Satan has many agents who are his tools against marriage. Erring spouses are usually unaware of the devices of the devil against their marriage and family. Some call it enjoyment not knowing that

---

[38] (Proverbs 16:3).

they are playing into the hands of marriage's worst enemy, the devil.

It has been noted that Satan attacks marriages because he wants to defile the marriage bed in order to eliminate the presence of God in the union. A successful marriage is likened to the body of Christ, the Church. Satan would not have any of that. He will adopt all possible mischief-making measures to destroy marriage. A marriage generally grows into a family which becomes the center of love expression. Family is the primary unit of the Church. In this nature of the family, it becomes the center for salvation and redemption. Satan would not allow these series of positives. He would prefer negatives, which are obviously at variance with divine requirements for marriage and family.

[Each of you in the family should look not only to your own interests, but also to the interest of other family members.]

Quest

1. Explain your understanding of the Trinitarian image of marriage using the role of love for an illumination of the idea.
2. How does the statement of Jesus in the text help in a better understanding of the Trinitarian image of the marriage union? (Matthew 19:4-6).

3. What business has Satan got in a marriage that makes him want to mess it up?
4. Name some ways by which Satan can attack a marriage with the intent of destroying it.
5. In the hospitality example, would you say that the wife made a mistake by giving shelter to her friend?
6. If you were in the place of the wife would you go ahead and offer your friend a place in your home?
7. Suggest the profile of the husband in the hospitality example i.e. what sort of person is the husband?
8. Describe an event you know that resembles the hospitality example.
9. Discuss the appropriateness of the utilization of both family discussion and seeking the counsel of the Lord.
10. What do you learn from the case of the movement of the Ark of God from Kiriath Jearim to Jerusalem?
11. How can marriage be related to mission in twos as described in Luke 10?

Memory Verse: "If you have any encouragement from being united with Christ, if any comfort from his love, if any fellowship with the Spirit, if any tenderness and compassion, then make my joy complete by being like-minded, having the same love, being one in spirit and purpose. Do nothing out of selfish ambition or vain conceit, but in humility consider others better than yourselves. Each of you should look not only to your own interests but also to the interest of others."[39]

---

[39] (Philippians 2:1-4)

Study Five

Topic: Searching For a Suitable Spouse

Text: When God created the first man, he put him in the Garden of Eden to tend and take care of it. Adam would end the day's work in the garden to return to his loneliness. He had no second human person to discuss the day's experiences at the place of work. It was very boring to live alone in the large Garden of Eden. In fact, God sympathized with Adam when he said, "It is not good for the man to be alone. I will make a helper suitable for him."[40] God then created the beasts and birds, which he brought to Adam to name them. These creatures had companions and helpers of their kind, "but for Adam no suitable helper was found."[41]

The indication is that God 'sought' for a wife for Adam but he could not find a suitable one for him. It was not that there were no helpers all over the place, but there was none that was suitable for Adam. Neither the animals, nor the trees in the Garden of Eden could be suitable helpers for Adam. There was only one suitable helper for Adam and only God could provide that suitable helper. "So the Lord God caused the man to fall into deep sleep and while he was sleeping, he took one of the man's ribs and closed up the

---

[40] (Genesis 2:18)
[41] (Genesis 2:20b)

place with flesh. The Lord God then made a woman from the rib he had taken out of the man, and he brought her to the man."[42]

This was the first marriage and it took place in the Garden of Eden. It is important that God made the woman with the rib of the man. The woman was therefore implicitly a part of the man. Adam himself said about the woman, "This is now bone of my bones and flesh of my flesh; she shall be called woman, for she was taken out of man."[43] God could as well have made the woman by any other method. The fact that he made her out of the body-part of the man informs on the fact that the woman was part of the man. The man and the woman were one flesh. In order to maintain the one flesh legacy of the union of the man and the woman, "a man will leave his father and mother and be united to his wife, and they will become one flesh."[44]

The first marriage at the Garden of Eden points to the need to end loneliness through getting a suitable wife. A suitable wife could not be found for the man in the Garden of Eden. This points to the need to search for a suitable wife. The search would be futile if God is not invited to lead in the search. God found the suitable wife for Adam and he is the one who is to find a suitable spouse for you. The use of the word "suitable" indicates that there are many spouses out there but only one is suitable. To get to that suitable spouse, there is

---

[42] (Genesis 2:21)
[43] (Genesis 2:21)

the important need to make an ordered search. There are three important areas of importance during the search for a suitable wife or husband:

(a) First seek the counsel of the Lord. "Houses and wealth are inherited from parents, but a prudent wife is from the Lord."[45] When you pray, you put God first in your plan as a guarantee that his will is done. God will give you a suitable spouse. "Commit to the Lord whatever you do, and your plans will succeed."[46]

(b) When you have prayed and you believe that God has revealed a suitable spouse, you will need to seek a confirmation from God and through the counsel of the people of God. "Whoever gives heed to instruction prospers, and blessed is he who trusts in the Lord."[47] The counsel of God and the counsel of the people of God are very important because "Plans fail for lack of counsel, but with many advisers they succeed."[48]

(c) Your success through counsel will then be further confirmed by the sincere divine love between you and your prospective spouse. Marriage is a lifetime union and as such, care must be taken to find that suitable spouse God has set apart for you and only you.

---

[44] (Genesis 2:24).
[45] (Proverbs 19:14)
[46] (Proverbs 16:3)
[47] (Proverbs 16:20)

If you fail to apply the described three tools in your search, it will be clear to you when you take someone's spouse as yours. "For lack of guidance a nation falls, but many advisers make victory sure."[49] Do not let carelessness rob you of your suitable helper. Your joy and peace at home will be sure if the Lord gives you a good spouse. Many people have failed-marriages because the spouse they have taken is unsuitable. When you do not get a suitable spouse, you have implicitly married another person's spouse. Such marriage will be unhealthy and will disintegrate. There is likely going to be divorce as many times as you marry an unsuitable spouse. In adopting the three steps in the search of a suitable spouse, do not let anyone take you hostage. Do not let that one who wants to have you by all means prevent you from going through the three search modalities. You must utilize these three modalities in eliminating unsuitable spouses. It is dangerous to depend on sex love in the choice of a suitable spouse. Sex love is deceptive. Marriage is not sex. Sex love must not be the route to marriage. Sex love does not endure. Marriage is a holy Trinitarian union that presents a foretaste of the kingdom of God.

Amnon son of David fell in love with Tamar, the beautiful sister of Absalom son of David. This was a sex love. He raped her. After raping Tamar, "Amnon hated her with intense hatred. In fact, he

---

[48] (Proverbs 15:22)
[49] (Proverbs 11:14)

hated her more than he had loved her."[50] Cohabitation is made possible by sex love. Cohabits may live together for many years but they may not be able to remain married for a few months. In many cases attempts by cohabits to get married never succeed because of the lack of divine matrimonial love. Sex love is what drives all immoral acts. Marriage through sex love will not have the Trinitarian image and it will also not endure. However, the grace of God cannot be ruled out for any reason because God will bless whosoever he wishes to bless. The important understanding here is that he who knows what is right and does not do it is sin. We cannot continue in sin that grace may abound. If you fail to adopt the three procedures of spousal search, you will not find a suitable spouse because God is not in your marriage plan. When you have not gotten a suitable spouse, and you marry anyone that comes across your way, then you have invested in trouble. You have thrown peace overboard and replaced it perpetual crisis and sadness. You cannot handle the mess. Be careful!

[Each of you in the family should look not only to your own interests, but also to the interest of other family members.]

Quest

1. What prompted God to seek a suitable helper for the man Adam?

---

[50] (2 Samuel 13:15)

2. How many suitable helpers were available for the first marriage?
3. Where did the first marriage take place?
4. God sought for a wife for Adam. Discuss.
5. Name and describe the three methods of spousal search.
6. Define sex love. What danger does it present in the search for a suitable spouse?
7. Why does marriage after cohabitation generally collapse relatively early despite a previous long period of cohabitation?
8. Discuss the action of Amnon against Tamar as described in 2 Samuel 13.
9. Explain the role of grace in the search for a suitable wife.
10. What warning is there in the text against ignoring God in spousal search on the grounds of the abundance of grace?
11. Enumerate the dangers of a failure to find a suitable spouse, and yet marriage takes place anyway.
12. Discuss 2 Corinthians 6:14-18.
13. In the search of a suitable wife it must be well-known that Satan has come to steal, kill and destroy while Jesus has come to give us life in its fullness. Discuss.

Memory Verse: "Commit to the Lord whatever you do, and your plans will succeed."[51]

---

[51] (Proverbs 16:3)

Study Six

Topic: Jew-Gentile Factor in Marriage

Text: The Gospel of our Lord Jesus Christ is the means by which God justifies people of all races and nationalities. All nations and all peoples are blessed through the object of faith, which is Jesus Christ. Since the righteous live by faith, it is reasonable for both Jews and Gentiles to have the benefit of receiving Jesus as Lord. Jesus Christ redeemed us in order that the blessing given to Abraham might come to the Gentiles through Jesus Christ, so that by faith we might receive the promise of the Holy Spirit. When one receives the Holy Spirit, that person becomes a son or daughter of God because he/she has the potential to obey God in everything.[52] There is therefore no condemnation for those who are in Christ Jesus because the Spirit of God has set us free from the bondage of disobedience. In this freedom, clannishness is summarily eliminated. Timothy was a Greek disciple of Jesus, whose mother was Jewish and a believer in Christ, and his father was a Greek.[53] Jews and non-Jews are all children of God through faith in Jesus Christ, and they marry each other according to the will of God. We all are baptized into Christ and our sins are washed away with the blood of Jesus. There is therefore,

---

[52] (Ezekiel 36:26-27). (Ezekiel 36:26-27).
[53] (Acts 16:1-2).

"neither Jew nor Greek, slave nor free, male nor female, for you are all one in Christ Jesus." [54]

If you are a Christian, and you wish to get married, do not allow nationality or race place constraints on the will of God for your life. The Lord can give you a spouse of any nationality or race if it is his perfect will. Do not be a stumbling block to the will of God. Christians all over the world, irrespective of their nationality or race, "are a chosen people, a royal priesthood, a holy nation, a people belonging to God, that you may declare the praises of him who called you out of darkness into his wonderful light. Once you were not a people, but now you are a people of God; once you had not received mercy, but now you have received mercy."[55] The problems people have in marriage take origin from their non-divine choice of spouse. There would be no significant marital problems if people allow God to find a suitable spouse for them. "Commit to the Lord whatever you do, and your plans will succeed."[56] He who finds a wife/husband finds what is good and receives favor from the Lord; houses and wealth are inherited from parents but a good spouse is from the Lord.[57]

In marriage some go out to seek the permissive will of God, while some others seek his perfect will. Those who seek the

---

[54] (Galatians 3:28, 1 Corinthians 12:13).
[55] (1 Peter 2:9-10).
[56] (Proverbs 16:3).
[57] (Proverbs 18:22, 19:14).

permissive will of God pray that God will give them a spouse on their own selfish conditions. They tell God, the nationality, the level of education, the profession, the desire of his own little group, the desire of his parents etc. When God gives such people the divine choice, they reject it. Then God gives them what they want to have according to his permissive will. To accept the permissive will of God in marriage is an investment in trouble. However, the person who seeks the perfect will of God allows God sufficient room for maneuver. God finds for the person a suitable spouse that is according to his perfect will. This marriage is usually successful and it is characterized by peace and harmony.

Those who seek the permissive will of God in marriage fail to realize that God said, "Do not team up with those who are unbelievers. How can goodness be a partner with wickedness? How can light live with darkness? What harmony can there be between Christ and the Devil? How can a believer be a partner with an unbeliever? And what union can there be between God's temple and idols? For we are the temple of the living God. As God said: 'I will live in them and walk among them. I will be their God and they will be my people. Therefore, come out of them and separate yourselves from them, says the Lord. Don't touch their filthy things and I will welcome you. And I will be your Father, and you will be my sons and daughters, says the Lord Almighty.'"[58] It is only God who knows

---

[58] (2 Corinthians 6:14-18 NLT).

the spouse that satisfies his requirements. You may think that a person is a Christian because he/she goes to Church. You may marry that person because he/she is of the same nationality or race. You cannot do God's work for him in spousal selection. You may get the person that meets your selfish conditions, but he/she could turn out to be a thorn in your flesh, exhibiting the worst type of immorality such that he/she is an agent of the devil in your home. You have to be careful and seek the perfect will of God in spousal search. The children of God belong in one place – a nation of God. They belong to Jesus and Jesus knows them by name. Therefore, if you belong to the nation of God, he will find a suitable spouse for you from his nation. Seek the perfect will of God in spousal search, and you will be glad you did. However, if you refuse his perfect will and desire his permissive will, you be preparing yourself for a bad marriage and an eventual marriage failure.

[Each of you in the family should look not only to your own interests, but also to the interest of other family members.]

Quest

1. How did Jews and Gentiles become equal persons before God?
2. Distinguish between the perfect and the permissive will of God.
3. Discuss Galatians 3:28, and 1 Corinthians 12:13.
4. How should a person go about the assignment of spousal search?
5. Timothy who was a very faithful disciple of Jesus, had parents of different nationalities. How did the marriage of his parents help the Gospel of Christ?
6. Explain how Job 1:6, and Job 2:1-2, should encourage you to ask God to give you a suitable spouse instead of your doing it by your own effort.
7. Discuss 2 Corinthians 6:14-18, illuminating strategies against any mistakes.
8. Give an example of a marriage contracted under the permissive will of God.
9. If you are married, please be kind to tell us how you found your spouse. Would you have done it differently now?
10. If you are not yet married and you plan to do so in future, how are you preparing and what should we expect from you in procedure for spousal search?

Memory Verse: Paul and Silas went first to Derbe and then to Lystra. There they met Timothy, a young disciple whose mother was a Jewish believer, but whose father was a Greek.[59]

---

[59] (Acts 16:1).

Study Seven

Topic: Procreation in Marriage

Text: God created us in his own image. He blessed us and said, "Be fruitful and increase in number; fill the earth and subdue it."[60] At marriage, spouses live a life of love because they imitate God who is love and lives a life of love. Love is what binds couples in perfect unity – generating the peace of Christ that rules in their hearts because they are members of one body. It is interesting that the spouses are not able to exhaust all the love God has given to them on themselves alone. The essential need for more recipients of their love corresponds with the divine injunction to be fruitful and increase in number. Marriage becomes fruitful when spouses begin to have children by their marriage. When children are born to them, these children become targets of parental love. Since love binds and unites, the emergent unit becomes a nuclear family enjoying a nuclear expression of love.[61] The family can be likened to the body of Christ in which there are many members working together as a unit.

The family is a secure place of rest, care and protection. It is the center for salvation and redemption. The family is a body of people bound together as a unit by love and called to a peaceful co-existence. When the first man, Adam lay with his wife, she became

---

[60] (Genesis 1:27-28)
[61] (Eke-Okoro 2003: Family Love and Spousal Equity, Dorrance Publishing Co. Pittsburg, PA, 2003).

pregnant and gave birth to a son. Eve, the first woman on earth said about her first son, "With the help of the Lord I have brought forth a man."[62] The birth of a child through the sexual union of a husband and his wife, shows that it is only when spouses work together as a unit that they can be fruitful. Sexual union implies that the man and the woman have become one flesh. This does not mean that they should take the honor for the child that is born through their union. Eve rightly noted that the baby she gave birth to was as a result of help from God. Children are a gift from God. They are a reward from the Lord.[63] Children are "like arrows in the hands of a warrior .... Blessed is the man whose quiver is full of them. They will not be put to shame when they contend with their enemies in the gate."[64] The family as a place of rest, care and protection is therefore fully armed by the Lord to defend and defeat external contending forces. In peace and unity, the family stands strong.

Children born to a family help to strengthen the bonds of love and unity. Children help marriages to endure. A fruitful marriage is procreating and generally stronger than a non-procreating marriage. This does not mean that a non-procreating marriage does not have what it takes to endure. In fact, it has no reason to go apart if love has been well-established between the spouses, especially in the Trinitarian style. Abraham and Sarah were married for over 50

---

[62] (Genesis 4:1)
[63] (Psalm 127:3)
[64] (Psalm 127:4-5)

years before they had their first child, Isaac. Isaac and Rebekah were married for about 20 years before they had their first children, the twin brothers, Esau and Jacob. These marriages were strongly bound by love and characterized by peace.

There is no evidence that the great missionary couple Aquila and Priscilla had any children. They were always traveling on missionary assignments. They were one of the most happily married couples ever. Priscilla and Aquila went to Syria and Ephesus with Apostle Paul on a missionary journey. In fact, during this journey, Paul left Priscilla and Aquila at Ephesus to minister to the people of Ephesus.[65] When Paul wrote to the Church at Rome, he greeted Priscilla and Aquila whom he referred to as his fellow workers in Christ. He remarked that Aquila and Priscilla had risked their lives for him and for the Gentile Churches.[66] By the time Paul wrote his first letter to the Church at Corinth, he was with Aquila and Priscilla who also included their warm greetings in the Lord for the Corinthian Church.[67] When Paul wrote his second letter to Timothy, he asked Timothy to greet Priscilla and Aquila.

From the standpoint that Priscilla and Aquila were always on missionary journey, one could suspect that they had no home. In fact, they had a Church in their home.[68] When the eloquent Jewish

---

[65] (Acts 18:18-19)
[66] (Romans 16:3-4)
[67] (1 Corinthian 16:19)
[68] (1 Corinthians 16:19).

preacher, Apollos was speaking of the baptism of John instead of Salvation through Jesus Christ, Priscilla and Aquila invited him to their home and explained the way of salvation more adequately to him.[69] Aquila and Priscilla's marriage was one that was completely devoted to serving Jesus and bringing honor to his name. They were a couple who effectively obeyed the command, "Whatever you do, work at it with all your heart, as working for the Lord, not for men, since you know that you receive an inheritance from the Lord as a reward. It is the Lord Christ you are serving."[70] It is when married couples recognize that the primary aim of their marriage is to contribute to the growth of the kingdom of God that their union becomes exciting and worthwhile. This is how a marriage becomes a ministry.

[Each of you in the family should look not only to your own interests, but also to the interest of other family members.]

Quest

1. Suggest reasons why God commanded humankind to be fruitful and increase in number.
2. What is the importance of having children in a marriage?
3. Define family and explain its importance.

---

[69] (Acts 18:25-26)
[70] (Colossians 3:23-24)

4. Since children come from a sexual union of spouses, why are they (children) seen as gifts from God?
5. Should infertility (childlessness) terminate a marriage?
6. Did infertility have a negative effect on the marriage of Isaac and Rebekah?
7. What efforts did Isaac and Rebekah make to end infertility? (Genesis 25:11-26).
8. Why is marriage regarded as a ministry?
9. Discuss the effectiveness of Priscilla and Aquila in missions for Christ.
10. Suggest who pastored the Church at the home of Aquila and Priscilla when they went on missionary journeys abroad?
11. Priscilla and Aquila were self-differentiated tent-makers who spent their married life preaching the Gospel of Jesus in different parts of the world. They also had a Church in their home. No mention was made of their having children in their marriage. Do you think that they had children, but that its lack of mention in the Bible was an inadvertent omission in their profile? **

** [In the Old Testament it is easy to know all members of a family but that is not the case in the New Testament. It is not even easy to determine who was married or not in the New Testament: In the holy family of Mary and Joseph, we know that after Jesus, more children were born to Joseph and Mary.⁷¹ Zebedee's sons, James and John were apostles of Jesus,⁷² but it was not indicated whether these disciples had their own wives and children. It is interesting that their mother obviously had a very important role in their Christian training. She knew the objective of the training she gave to her children. In pursuant of that objective, she came to Jesus with her two sons, knelt down before him and requested, "Grant that one of these two sons of mine may sit at your right and the other at your left in your kingdom."⁷³ She was a great woman of faith. She was among the women who had followed Jesus from Galilee and provided his needs.⁷⁴ During the passion of Christ, she was among the women who watched from a distance. Evangelist Philip had four unmarried daughters who prophesied.⁷⁵ Although Philip's wife was not mentioned, the evidence is that she played an important role in the Christian training of her daughters. The Lord's brothers, and Peter had believing wives but their children were not named.⁷⁶ Jesus healed Simon Peter's mother-in-law of high fever.⁷⁷ There are indications, however, that some apostles like Paul did not have a wife. Mary Magdalene, Martha and Mary, the sisters of Lazarus, may not have been married, but they were heroic people of faith].

---

[71] (Mark 3:31-35, Mark 6:3)
[72] (Matthew 4:21-22)
[73] Matthew 20:20-21
[74] Matthew 27:55-56
[75] Acts 21:8-9
[76] (1 Corinthians 9:5)

Memory Verse: "Be fruitful and increase in number; fill the earth and subdue it."[78]

---

[77] (Mark 1:29-31, Luke 4:38-39)].
[78] (Genesis 1:27-28).

Study Eight

Topic: Socialization of Children

Text: Children are a gift from God to husband and wife. They have been given to strengthen marriage relationship and as a part of the growth of the family, which is not only the primary unit of the Church, but also a part of the growing kingdom of God. There is great joy in a family when these children arrive to grace a marriage. Children represent an important investment for parents and also for the kingdom of God. They represent the future of a nation. In order not to lose the benefits of having children, they must be properly socialized. When they arrive in the world, they are honest in purity and in all that it takes to enter the kingdom of God. At times we see these children being born to people who are not able to take good care of them. Some parents without any bad intention make great mistakes in the way they train their children. This error is mostly due to the choice of disciplinary measures that are inadequate. "Discipline your son, for in that there is hope; do not be a willing party to his death."[79]

Death is what the devil has purposed for children because they are seen by him as a threat, being the future of a great nation and above all, of the kingdom of God. The devil's objective is to steal, kill and destroy these children. He engages in manipulating

---
[79] (Proverbs 19:18)

their minds in order to lead them to do evil thereby, stealing them from their parents and finally destroying them. "Discipline your son, and he will give you peace; he will bring delight to your soul."[80] It is when you fail to discipline children properly that you play into the hands of the devil. The parents of Jesus took him to the house of God for worship. When he got missing, they found him in the house of God. He said to his parents, "Why were you searching for me? Didn't you know I had to be in my Father's house?"[81] This is consistent with, "Train a child in the way he should go, and when he is old he will not turn from it."[82] It will also be noted that parents may do a good job at home in training their children, but when these children come in contact with other children who have not received good family training, things go bad.

Socialization of children is not solely the duty of parents. The training of children involves the whole community, the whole nation and special agencies. Parents may do an excellent job at home in giving sound biblical training to their children, but when they are sent out to other agents of socialization things go bad. The evidence is that the best training that parents give to their children are Bible-based. Other agents of socialization that do not draw upon biblical instructions fail to meet the goals of child training. There are agencies who allow free practice of religion but since such religion is

---

[80] (Proverbs 29:17)
[81] (Luke 2:49)
[82] (Proverbs 22:6)

not organized the kids are not able to benefit from it because, they need guidance. For instance in the public school system (Primary School to High School level) the free practice of religion offered children without guidance by a chaplain is simply meaningless. This is tantamount to no freedom to practice religion in the schools. The Bible is a spiritual book that is not even easy for mature adults to understand without the guidance of the Holy Spirit. How on earth can we expect these children to gain anything from the purported free practice of one's faith in the public school system without guidance? Many public bodies like the Senate, Parliament and the Army have chaplains that give guidance in matters of faith, but children who should need more guidance in matters of faith are left out in our public schools to satanic mind-manipulation. It is very important to submit our public school system to God. Chaplains should be employed to guide moral education in our public schools. We need to resist the devil there, and he will flee from our children. If we come near to God, he will come near to us.[83]

In relation to offering quality training to our children at school, Satan is presenting himself as the goliath threatening to cause havoc. People are forming battle lines but they are not fighting. Someone needs to come out like David to challenge goliath and kill him. We cannot keep arguing on prayers at school and fail to do something realistic when the devil is taking over at our schools.

---

[83] (James 4:7-10).

Things are going bad and people do not want to stand up against the evil that is threatening the future of our great nation. Thank God for prayer warriors all over this nation. People of faith are fighting from the grandstand on their knees to stop goliath from threatening the future of this nation. The teachers are the Israelite soldiers; the students are the future hopes of Israel; goliath is Satan trying to destroy the hope and future of Israel. What we are lacking is a David to stand up to face Satan and destroy him.

Moses said to the people of Israel, "This day I call heaven and earth as witnesses against you that I have set before you life and death, blessings and curses. Now choose life, so that you and your children may live and that you may love the Lord your God, listen to his voice, and hold fast to him. For the Lord is your life, and he will give you many years in the land he swore to give to your fathers, Abraham, Isaac, and Jacob."[84] The fathers of our great nation founded it on trust in God. They established public schools that trained our children, instilling in them the fear of God and respect for law and order. The standard has fallen because goliath has taken over, threatening with cults, sex and making the schools warfronts in which our children are gunned down. The carnage has been taken to the streets and homes and terror is all over the place because God has been ignored and left out of our schools. There is no David to challenge the goliath as the decay of the school system progresses to

---

[84] (Deuteronomy 30:19-20)

a doomsday. It is surprising that parents are sort of hypnotized and resigned to fate in this matter. The "I don't care attitude" is taking a toll that is becoming difficult to contain. In such a time as this we need someone to stand up to the situation.

You see the trouble we are in. Our public schools lie in ruins. Come let us build the walls and we will no longer be a disgrace. The gracious hand of our God is upon us. Let us start rebuilding our public schools. The God of heaven will give us success through our Lord Jesus Christ.[85] It is not by might nor by power, but by the Spirit of Jesus. What are you O mighty mountain before the great people of our nation? President Reagan called for the pulling down of the evil wall in Berlin, and it went down. The satanic wall in the public school system must go down and the people of God will regain their freedom to take Jesus to the children who represent the future of our great nation.

[Each of you in the family should look not only to your own interests, but also to the interest of other family members.]

Quest

1. How may children born to a family be a rewarding investment to their parents?
2. Discuss the failure of discipline in some families.

---

[85] (Nehemiah 2:17-20)

3. Explain the following scripture, "Discipline your son, for in that there is hope; do not be a willing party to his death."
4. Suggest the best agent of socialization for children.
5. Evidence has shown that Bible-based training is the most rewarding for children. How best can this be done in our homes?
6. Discuss the concept of balanced-training of children in relation to Ephesians 6:1-4.
7. What can be done to resist the breakdown of discipline in our public schools?
8. Discuss the origin of the present mess in our public schools.
9. Has the system accepted defeat as things seem to have turned topsy-turvy in the schools?
10. From the text, who is the goliath and who are the Israelites in our public school system?
11. Discuss the proposal for the appointment of chaplains to guide moral education in our public schools.
12. Discuss a possible emergence of a "David" to kill the goliath in our public school system.

Memory Verse: David said to the Philistine, "You come against me with sword and spear and javelin, but I come against you in the name of the Lord Almighty, the God of the armies of Israel whom you have defied."[86]

---

[86] (1 Samuel 17:45)

Study Nine

Topic: An Exploration of Peace in Marriage and Family

Text: The most important thing sought after in marriage and family is peace. Peace implies a cordial relationship with your neighbor in which fear does not exist. The purpose of love is to generate peace. Love and peace go together in the affairs of humankind. It is therefore not surprising that God is love and Jesus is the Prince of Peace. Humankind cannot have peace in a condition of sin. Sin takes away peace. In order to restore peace God loved the world and gave his only begotten Son, so that anyone who believes in him should not perish but have eternal life.[87] It is gratifying that the Prince of Peace was given to us to give us peace. The Gospel has it that anyone who believes in Jesus should not perish but have everlasting life. The reason for a lack of peace is related to the thoughts of the danger of perishing. To envisage danger in life is a single most important factor that takes away peace. You do not have peace because you might have lost hope in a person who should have loved you but is now hostile to you. That person who used to love you now hates you. He/she knows your weak points, where to attack and destroy you. Peace is gone, and you try to work for a restoration of peace.

---

[87] (John 3:16)

There are many other factors that can take away your peace. When peace is threatened or taken away, the best way to restore it is to go back to the Prince of Peace who gives peace in abundance. Your prayer to the Prince of Peace will eliminate all obstacles to peace and restore cordial friendly relations. Jesus who is the Prince of Peace said to his disciples, "I have told you these things, so that in me you may have peace. In the world you have trouble. But take heart! I have overcome the world."[88] There can be no peace when you are in trouble. "God has called us to live in peace."[89] Anything that goes contrary to the will of God will result in trouble. It is the will of God that we live in peace. Therefore, any disruption of peace will result in trouble. Trouble comes from the world while peace comes from God our Father and from our Lord Jesus Christ.[90] Those who want peace must get it from the right source. In marriage, peace is already guaranteed through its Trinitarian nature. However, spouses who ignore goodness in their relationship invite trouble to replace their God-given peace.

Spouses should have faith in the desire of God to make them live in peace. They should know that they can have peace with God and with their partner if they are justified through faith in Jesus Christ. Peace with God means peace with people because God is in control. It does not matter what you are going through, if you have

---

[88] (John 16:33).
[89] (1 Corinthians 7:15)
[90] (Roman 1:7)

peace with God through Jesus Christ, it will be all right. Spouses, you should know that Jesus Christ himself is your peace! He has made the two of you into one flesh and has destroyed the barrier of any potential hostility.[91] Your marriage has become God's household built on the foundation of the Prince of Peace. In Jesus both of you have been joined together to become a dwelling in which God lives by his Spirit.[92] The peace of God which transcends all understanding will be with you if you make it your abounding duty to think about, and also put to practice in your marriage and family, whatever is true, whatever is noble, whatever is admirable, excellent, or praiseworthy.[93]

Do not pick a quarrel with your spouse. The peace of Christ should rule in your hearts, since as members of one body you are called to peace in a holy matrimony. Do not argue with your spouse in order to come out a winner. It is never helpful to drag a point for too long because you consider yourself to be in a more comfortable position. If you press too much, you would be attacking love and blocking the emergence of peace. As members of one flesh, how on earth would you run down your spouse? Be aware that you are working against yourself when you enjoy putting down on your spouse. Whatever is not good for you is also not good for your spouse. Do not discuss your spouse negatively with other people.

---

[91] (Ephesians 2:14)
[92] (Ephesians 2:15-22)
[93] (Philippians 4:7-9)

Seek the counsel of God and determine the right course of action in your spousal relationship. God will never leave you nor forsake you. He will give you the guidance that restores peace and harmony in your marriage and family. Finally, in your marriage do not let love and faithfulness leave you. Hold tightly to them and imprint them in your heart. Then you will win favor and a good name in the sight of God and all people, especially in the sight of your spouse and members of your family. Trust in the Lord with all your heart and lean not on your own understanding; in all your ways acknowledge the Lord and he will make your paths straight and you will see your marriage endure in peace and harmony.[94]

[Each of you in the family should look not only to your own interests, but also to the interest of other family members.]

Quest
1. Explain the relationship between love and peace.
2. Discuss in relation to marriage and family, "Let the peace of Christ rule in your hearts since as members of one body you are called to peace." (Colossians 3:15)/ "God has called us to live in peace." (1 Corinthians 7:15)
3. Attempt a personal definition of peace.
4. Give an instance of a breakdown of peace in your family.

---
[94] (Proverbs 3:1-6).

5. How may spouses and their family derive encouragement from the fact that Jesus is the Prince of Peace? (Isaiah 9:6).
6. In what ways can spouses and their family strengthen their relationship with Jesus both at home and in the Church?
7. How may spouses or other members of their family disrupt peace?
8. Suggest ways by which peace may be sustained in a marriage and in the family.
9. Can one have peace with Jesus when he has no peace with his/her spouse?

Memory Verse: Let us therefore make every effort to do what leads to peace and mutual edification.[95]

---

[95] (Romans 14:19)

Study Ten

Topic: Family as a Functional Unit

Text: The family can be likened to the body of Christ, which is the Church. In fact, the family is the primary unit of the Church of Christ, functionally characterized as a place of rest, care, protection, salvation and redemption. Like the early Pentecostal family of believers who formed into a Church, family members are duty bound to stay together as a unit having everything in common. The family altar should be an important uniting tool for the family as they eat together with glad and sincere hearts praising God and enjoying the favor of not only family members but also of people from outside the family. The Lord will add to the number of family members through procreation and other means.[96]

All family members should be one in heart and mind. In a family, no member claims his/her possessions as his own but members share everything they own. There should be no needy family member as they make Jesus the Lord of the family, using the family altar to ensure the centrality of Christ in all family affairs. Resources of the family should be made available to any member who is in need.[97] In order to fulfill the law of Christ, which is the foundation of love on which the family is established, family

---

[96] (Acts 2:42-47)
[97] (Acts 4:32-37)

members carry each other's burdens.[98] A helpful advice to family members is, "Do not be weary in doing good, for at the proper time we will reap a harvest if we do not give up. Therefore, as we have opportunity, let us do good to all people, especially to those who belong to the family of believers."[99]

Family members should be like-minded, having the same sincere love, being one in spirit and purpose. They should not do anything out of selfish ambition or vain conceit, but should in humility, consider others better than themselves.[100] Members of the family should always communicate in order to increase the strength of their relationship. Communication gaps need to be bridged as soon as they occur in order not to disfellowship any family member. Evidence has shown that communication gap is increasing in many modern families because of infidelity and other sins that break the hearts of family members. In some cases we see husband and wife sleeping in different rooms; husband and wife live in different apartments in the same city and children shuttle from one parent's home to the other parent's home. Some parents poison the minds of the innocent children with negative stories about the other parent. This should not be the case. These children are given to strengthen marriage. Their minds should not be polluted with blackmail but with good stuff so that they would be in a better position to bring

---

[98] (Galatians 6:2)
[99] (Galatians 6:9-10).
[100] (Philippians 4:1-4)

their parents together again. "By wisdom a house is built, and through understanding it is established; through knowledge its rooms are filled with rare and beautiful treasures."[101]

Trustworthy actions are expected from all members of the family and no one should count himself/herself better than the other. You should not seek only your own interest, but also the interest of others. Family members should have compassion one for another and if any member of the family has a message of encouragement for another member or for the whole family, he/she should speak it without delay. This is the way to move forward in family relations without leaving anyone behind. "We who are strong ought to bear with the failings of the weak and not to please ourselves. Each of us should please his neighbor for his good, to build him up. For even Christ did not please himself but, as it is written: 'The insults of those who insult you have fallen on me.' .... May the God who gives endurance and encouragement give you a spirit of unity among yourselves as you follow Christ, so that with one heart and mouth you may glorify the God and Father of our Lord Jesus Christ. Accept one another, then, just as Christ accepted you, in order to bring praise to God."[102] Every member of the family should be self-differentiated. A self-differentiated person like Jesus Christ our perfect example, is a very reliable person who says what he/she

---

[101] (Proverbs 24:3-4).
[102] (Romans 15:1-3, 5-7).

wishes to say, and does what he/she wishes to do, which are trustworthy actions leading to the edification of family members.

[Each of you in the family should look not only to your own interests, but also to the interest of other family members.]

Quest

1. Define family, and state the sources of its enrichment.
2. In your own opinion, explain how a family altar can be a very important uniting force in the family?
3. Who should be the priest of the family, mom or dad?
4. What are the similarities between a Church and a family?
5. What could be the causes of conflict in a family?
6. Explain trustworthy action.
7. How may effective communication strengthen family relations?
8. What is a communication gap and how could such a gap be bridged?
9. Define self-differentiation. How does self-differentiation of family members help in family relations?
10. Is there any member of your family who is not self-differentiated? How have you been able to help that one to become a more reliable person?

Memory Verse: Let us not become weary in doing good, for at the proper time we will reap a harvest if we do not give up.[103]

---

[103] (Galatians 6:9)

Study Eleven

Topic: Restoration of Cordial Relations

Text: In all human relations, there are times when things go bad and people are no longer relating well. This is a part of life, but efforts must be made to restore working relations. Satan, the enemy of peace will always try to cause a mess but the people of God are not unaware of his devices. He must not be allowed to have a foothold in our marital and family relations. He is a liar that must be resisted. "Be self-controlled and alert. Your enemy, the devil prowls around like a roaring lion looking for someone to devour. Resist him, standing firm in the faith, because you know that your brothers throughout the world are undergoing the same kind of suffering."[104] This means that when things are no longer smooth as they used to be in your relationship, it a red flag showing that the devil wants to steal, kill and destroy. You will need to seek the help of Jesus our Savior who has come to give us abundant life.

Jesus is always ready to fight for you against the devil and restore peace and harmony in your relationship. You are not the only person experiencing satanic disruption in your relationship. He is causing his mischief in the relationship of brothers and sisters all over the world. You do not therefore begin to apportion blame on each other, but recognize that Satan is at work and you should begin to

---

[104] (1 Peter 5:8-9)

resist him with your spiritual armor. It calls for your participation in the divine nature that helps you to escape the corruption in the world caused by evil desires. In your relationship, "make every effort to add to your faith goodness; and to goodness, knowledge; and to knowledge, self-control; and to self-control, perseverance; and to perseverance, godliness; and to godliness, brotherly kindness; and to brotherly kindness, love."[105] In spousal and family relations, there is the important need for you to possess and grow in these qualities.

Prayer is usually the first step that has to be taken when you notice that things are going bad. If you have not been praying or you have not been constant in prayers, then you should get back to serious prayers to invite the Holy Spirit into what you are passing through. Until you talk to God about what you are passing through, you should not expect any breakthrough. Prayers can lift you up to the mountaintop of victory. Spouses need to know that in the Trinitarian image of their union, any negligence of God would obviously result in instability in marital relations. Sin is a non-participant in the divine nature. Since you know that God is part of your marital union, sin should not be allowed. Righteous and trustworthy actions will sustain divine role in marriage and family affairs. You should know that the devil allows sin to come into marital union in order to minimize divine presence. You need the family altar to strengthen your union through prayers and knowledge

---

[105] (2 Peter 1:4-7)

of the word of God. This is how you add goodness to your faith; and to goodness, knowledge. Knowledge of the word of God will generate self-control etc.[106] Fasting will help to increase the effectiveness of your prayers. The Holy Spirit will then intervene in your hearts and normalize relations.

The presence of the Holy Spirit is an invitation to everyone to embrace compassion. Job's perseverance resulted in victory because the Lord is full of compassion and mercy.[107] The Lord is with you go ahead and generate harmony in your relationship through trustworthy actions. If you have any message of encouragement for your spouse, do not delay in speaking it. This will help you to bridge any communication gap that might have arisen during a problem. Talking to your spouse no matter what, is the tool that will open lines of communication. If there is any apology to render or a confession to make, do not delay. These are helpful tools that will stimulate the restoration of cordial relationship. You will come to an understanding and things will be all right again. Remember that God has called you to peace, therefore seek peace with all the energy that God has given to you. No longer allow the devil to cause the mess again in your relationship. If you are strong, then you ought to bear with the failings of the weak, and not to please yourself. Each of you should please his partner for his good, to build him/her up. Christ

---

[106] (2 Peter 1:4-7)
[107] (James 5:11)

Jesus did not please himself, but he rather allowed the insults that should fall on us to fall on his person.[108] Stop highlighting the weak points of your partner, but find the good side of him/her and generate compassion and encouragement for him/her.

You must know that you have to work on your marriage before it can succeed. There is no perfect person and there is no perfect marriage. You must be determined to work on your marriage and aim at perfection in the future. You and your marriage have to pass through fire before you can come forth as gold. We all carry baggages into marriage but we have to deal with each others faults with commonsense and with wisdom. Nothing should separate you from the love of God given to you by God himself at marriage. Hang in there and refuse to submit to devil's trick to dislodge you from the matrimonial union, which God has sealed with his love. Never take away your love from your spouse because he/she has messed up. Help to prop him/her up and thereby provide the modalities for necessary healing to occur. It will eventually be all right and you will be in a good position to give testimonies of the goodness of the Lord. No cross, no crown is also true in marriage. The conclusion is that you must not ignore God in your relationship. Prayerfully seek in love, the counsel of the Lord and if necessary, the counsel of the people of God and your victory will be sure.

---

[108] (Romans 15:1-3)

[Each of you in the family should look not only to your own interests, but also to the interest of other family members.]

Quest

1. Does a disagreement in marital relations mean an abomination?
2. What is the spiritual origin of spousal and family problems?
3. Why does the devil attack the Trinitarian image of spousal relationship?
4. In what ways may spouses resist attempts to dislodge the three persons of the marital union?
5. Discuss how prayer intervention can bring about a breakthrough in marital and family problems.
6. What is the role of the Holy Spirit in the restoration of cordial relations that might have been disrupted by the devil through sin?
7. Explain the importance of perseverance and self-control?
8. Discuss Malachi 2:16 (c.f. Matthew 19:4-6).
9. What is the importance of the divine image in all you do in your married life?
10. In your opinion, does the church have any role in settling marital disputes?
11. If the Church has any role to play, at what point should they come in to help?

Memory Verse: Finally, all of you, live in harmony with one another; be sympathetic, love as brothers and sisters, be compassionate and humble. Do not repay evil with evil or insult with insult, but with blessing, because to this you were called so that you may inherit a blessing.[109]

---

[109] (1 Peter 3:8-9)

Study Twelve

Topic: Effects of Mortality on Marriage and Family

Text: In the scriptures, we see famine playing a significant role in the determination of the destiny of people. Famine caused the movement of Abram from the Promised Land of Canaan to Egypt.[110] Another incident of famine in the Promised Land caused Isaac to leave for Gerar of the Philistines.[111] The movement of Jacob's family from Canaan to Egypt in a bid to escape death from severe famine is by far the most well-known of famine-related flights of people. The movement of Jacob's family to Egypt where his very young son Joseph had become the prime minister of Egypt is scripturally important. People may plan evil against you but God can convert it into good. It was in the foreign land of Egypt that the family of Jacob developed into the nation of Israel, which we know today. The sojourn of the Israelites in Egypt was the modality through which God the Father revealed himself to his creation with unprecedented miracles. The miracles convincingly revealed the invincible power of God. God had raised up Pharaoh for the very purpose, of showing him his divine power and his great name to be proclaimed in all the earth.[112]

---

[110] (Genesis 12:10).
[111] (Genesis 26:1).
[112] (Exodus 9:16).

In this study, we shall yet learn about another severe famine that has determined the destiny of all of us. During the days when Israel had no kings and were ruled by judges, famine caused Elimelech and his family to leave Bethlehem in Judea to the foreign land of Moab. Elimelech arrived in the land of Moab with his wife and their two sons Mahlon and Kilion. The joy they derived from escape from the severe famine was short-lived because, Elimelech died and Naomi became a widow. Her sons Mahlon and Kilion married beautiful Moabite girls named Orpah and Ruth. Ten years after the family of Elimelech left Bethlehem of Judah to Moab, disaster struck again as Naomi's two sons died and left their new wives desolate and widowed. Naomi was now living with her daughters-in-law. She could only derive comfort from her daughters-in-law, Orpah and Ruth. It was no real comfort for her as frustration steered on her face.

Naomi advised her daughters-in-law to return to their Moabite parents since their husbands had died. Orpah returned to her parents' home, but Ruth refused to leave Naomi because she loved her mother-in-law and had compassion in her heart for her. Ruth told her mother-in-law, Naomi, "Don't urge me to leave you or to turn back from you. Where you go I will go, and where you stay I will stay. Your people will be my people, and your God will be my God. Where you die I will die, and there I will be buried. May the Lord deal with me, be it ever so severely if anything but death separates you and me."[113] We see that Ruth returned to Bethlehem with Naomi. She became Naomi's source of comfort after the death of her husband and sons.

On arrival in Bethlehem, it was difficult for people to recognize Naomi because what she was going through had taken a toll on her and minimized her once pleasant personality. The whole town of Bethlehem was stirred when Naomi arrived. Her compatriot women were so surprised at her sad-looking appearance that they asked each other, "Can this be Naomi?" She rebuffed her compatriots who called her Naomi. Naomi preferred being called Mara, which means "bitter." Naomi said, "The Almighty has made life very bitter. I went away full, but the Lord has brought me back empty. Why call me Naomi? The Lord has afflicted me; the Almighty has brought misfortune upon me."[114]

Naomi and her Moabite daughter-in-law Ruth began to face the realities of life in Bethlehem. Ruth came in contact with Boaz, who was a close relation of her late father-in-law Elimelech. Boaz invoked traditional privileges and married Ruth. She conceived and gave birth to a son named Obed.[115] The women of Bethlehem said, to Naomi, "Praise be the Lord, who this day has not left you without a kinsman-redeemer. May he become famous throughout Israel! He will renew your life and sustain you in your old age. For your

---

[113] (Ruth 1:16-17).
[114] (Ruth 1:20-21).

daughter-in-law, who loves you and who is better to you than seven sons, has given him birth."[116] Obed the son of Ruth became the father of Jesse, and Jesse became the Father of David. It will be noted that Jesus Christ our Lord and Savior is from the line of David.

This study shows that death of spouse or children should not mean a state of hopelessness. God can use even death to bring about his purpose for your life. Oftentimes, people have misinterpreted death. Why should you cringe because your beloved is no more here with you? Remember that, "Precious in the sight of the Lord is the death of his saints."[117] Prophet Isaiah wrote: "The righteous perish and no one ponders it in his heart; devout men are taken away and no one understands that the righteous are taken away to be spared from evil. Those who walk uprightly enter into peace; they find rest as they lie in death."[118] Christians who are not worried about death prefer to be away from this body of ours and be at home with the Lord. "So we make it our goal to please him, whether we are at home in the body or away from it."[119]

[Each of you in the family should look not only to your own interests, but also to the interest of other family members.]

---

[115] (Ruth 4:17).
[116] (Ruth 4:14-15).
[117] (Psalm 116:15).
[118] (Isaiah 57:1-2).

Quest

1. Give examples of famines that have caused people of God to move from their place of primary assignment to a foreign land?
2. Elimelech and his family were citizens of which city in Judah?
3. After how many years in the land of Moab did Naomi lose her two sons through death? (Ruth 1:4).
4. Name the daughters-in-law of Naomi.
5. Why did Naomi decide to leave the land of Moab and return to her home in Bethlehem of Judah?
6. Why did Naomi persuade her daughters-in-law to return to their Moabite parents?
7. Discuss the responses of Orpah and Ruth to the requests of their mother-in-law to return to their parents.
8. Illuminate the love of Ruth for her mother-in-law. (Ruth 1:16-17, 4:15).
9. "The women exclaimed, 'Can this be Naomi.'" Discuss.
10. Discuss the scriptural importance of the marriage of Ruth to Boaz. (Ruth 4:13-22).
11. Suggest why Elimelech and his family did not have it nicely at Moab. Could it be that they did not first seek the counsel of the Lord before they left Bethlehem for the land of Moab?

---

[119] (2 Corinthians 5:8).

12. Why did Naomi not go into a second marriage after the death of her husband?
13. If you were in the place of Naomi, how would you respond to the difficult experiences of death in her family?
14. On return to Bethlehem from the land of Moab, would you expect that all the people of Bethlehem sympathized with Naomi?

Memory Verse: But Ruth replied, "Don't urge me to leave you or to turn back from you. Where you go I will go, and where you stay I will stay. Your people will be my people and your God my God."[120]

---

[120] (Ruth 1:16).

Study Thirteen

Topic: Divorce

Text: Marriage and divorce are primarily used to describe our relationship with God. When you love the Lord and walk according to his precepts, it can be said that you are married to God. We are the bride of Jesus and he is the bridegroom.[121] When a person obeys God and does his will, that one is married to God. However, if a person is disobedient to the commandments of God and lives a life of sin, that one is divorced by God.[122] God gave faithless Israel a certificate of divorce and sent her away because of her adulteries.[123] When a person leaves God and worships an idol, that one commits adultery and he/she is divorced from God. It can be seen that our relationships take their bearing from our relationship with God. We must first of all love God before we are able to love any other person. We love God with the love he has given to us. It is when our love for God is wholehearted that we can have meaningful love with our neighbor. God is love and love comes from God. If you cannot love God, where can you obtain the love with which to love your neighbor?

We therefore need to be married first to God before we can marry a human person. It is when we are truly married to God that

---

[121] (Mark 2:19-20).
[122] (Isaiah 50:1).

our marriage with a human person can endure. "Marriage should be honored by all, and the marriage bed kept pure, for God will judge the adulterer and all the sexually immoral."[124] It can be seen that the greatest enemy of marriage endurance is adultery. In our relationship with God, the worst sin against God is spiritual adultery in which a person has another god in the place of the Almighty God. Our relationship with God should not experience any hitches at all because every other action of man would be useless without a wholehearted belief in God. It is when we are married to God that we can function effectively well on earth. After all, it is in Christ we live and have our being. If we love God wholeheartedly, we will know that infidelity is devil's tool to destroy marriage. When a person breaks faith with his/her spouse through infidelity, almost everything would be messed up. Infidelity is a breach of trust and a disruption of divine plan in which, "The two become one flesh" in marriage.

When you sleep with another person in infidelity, you make yourself one flesh with that strange person. Apostle Paul remarked that everything is permissible, but not everything is beneficial. Do not allow anything to master you. "The body is not meant for sexual immorality, but for the Lord, and the Lord for the body. By his power, God raised the Lord from the dead, and he will raise us also.

---

[123] (Jeremiah 3:8).
[124] (Hebrews 13:4).

Do you know that your bodies are members of Christ himself? Shall I then take the members of Christ and unite them with a prostitute? Never! Do you not know that he who unites himself with a prostitute is one with her in body? For it is said, 'The two will become one flesh.' But he who unites himself with the Lord is one with him in spirit. Flee from sexual immorality. All other sins a man commits are outside his body, but he who sins sexually sins against his own body. Do you not know that your body is the temple of the Holy Spirit, who is in you, whom you have received from God? You are not your own; you were bought with a price. Therefore honor God with your body."[125]

The sin of infidelity has now become more dangerous than ever. This is because deadly sexually transmitted diseases are so prevalent that you could be digging your own grave when you involve yourself in sexual immorality. Sexually transmitted diseases have a multiplier effect. You would invariably spread such diseases to other people including members of your household. Protective measures are not divine and cannot therefore completely shield you away from those deadly infections. Leave your pants up! Why destroy yourself, members of your family, and your marital union through this senseless animal behavior. There is need for self-control. Time has passed when men cheat on their wives with reckless abandon and yet get away with it. Both men and women who engage in adultery have

---

[125] (1 Corinthians 6:12-20).

equally cheated on each other and their actions should be regarded as equal and a serious breach of marriage contract. Spouses should exercise self-control and avoid falling into the hands of Satan whose sole aim is to destroy your marriage and your very life. Please exercise self-control and allow sincere love to control your relationship. Do not allow Satan to outwit you with his destructive schemes. Do not break the heart of your spouse and disorganize your children through infidelity. Why should you do that?

Another important aspect of your spousal relationship is the grace to remain married for better or for worse. It is a very important part of your marriage covenant. A marriage covenant is an agreement between spouses. This agreement is witnessed by God and people of God. You are duty-bound to honor the agreement under all circumstances. You should not break faith with your spouse; your marriage covenant disallows it. The Lord has made both of you one, and you belong to God in flesh and in spirit. God has said, "I hate divorce."[126] Since Jesus forgives all our sins and accepts us back into his kingdom, spouses should likewise forgive each others sins and remain married.

Jesus said to the Pharisees, "Moses permitted you to divorce your wives because your hearts were hard. But it was not this way from the beginning."[127] Moses had permitted a man to write a

---

[126] (Malachi 2:16).
[127] (Matthew 19:8).

certificate of divorce and send his wife away. But Jesus told the Pharisees, "It was because your hearts were hard that Moses wrote you this law. But at the beginning of creation God made them male and female. For this reason a man will leave his father and mother and be united to his wife, and the two will become one flesh. So they are no longer two, but one. Therefore, what God has joined together let not man separate. ...... Anyone who divorces his wife and marries another woman commits adultery against her. And if she divorces her husband and marries another man, she commits adultery."[128]

[Each of you in the family should look not only to your own interests, but also to the interest of other family members.]

Quest

1. Discuss the spiritual imagery of marriage and divorce in our relationship with God the Father.
2. Explain how a cordial relationship with God becomes a guarantee for enduring spousal relationship.
3. Discuss the importance of Hebrews 13:4 in the achievement of a happy and enduring marriage.
4. How does marital infidelity breach marriage covenant and expose life to danger?

---

[128] (Mark 10:5-9, 11, 12).

5. Sexually transmitted diseases have a multiplier effect. Explain.
6. Discuss the spiritual implications of 1 Corinthians 6:12-20.
7. Why are protective measures against sexually transmitted diseases not a guarantee for safety?
8. The enemy of marriage is Satan. Discuss in the context of John 10:10.
9. Discuss Malachi 2:13-16 and relate your discussion to Mark 10:5-12.
10. Why did Moses allow divorce despite the fact that it is not God's plan from the beginning?

Memory Verse: Therefore what God has joined together let man not separate.[129]

---

[129] (Mark 10:9).

Study Fourteen

Topic: Illumination of Spousal Equality

Text: Marital problems are in many cases related to spousal misconception of parity in their relationship. This study will illuminate spousal equality through equality in Christ. Jesus said, "All of you are on the same level as brothers and sisters."[130] In the new life we live in Christ, it doesn't matter if you are a Jew or Gentile, man or woman, circumcised or uncircumcised, barbaric, uncivilized, slave or free. Jesus Christ is all that matters, and he lives in all of us.[131] It does not matter whether you are a husband or a wife. What matters is that Christ lives in you. When Christ lives in both wife and husband, they are equal. Christ is what matters in this comparison. You look out for the presence of Christ and once you can see Christ in a person, that person is your equal because Christ is Christ.

It is important that we understand what equality in Christ means; we are all created in the image of God, which guarantees human dignity for all God's creation. This dignity must be sustained in our dealings with each other. Equality in Christ implies that everyone should be given equal opportunity in life. There should also be mutual respect and submission to one another in order to prove our sincerity in the maintenance of human dignity and peaceful coexistence. In marriage and family, wives should be submissive and

---

[130] (Matthew 23:8b NLT).

respectful to their husbands, while husbands should love their wives and not be harsh with them. Husbands should be considerate in dealing with their wives and also treat them with respect as the weaker partner and also as a child of God - who like the husband is an heir to the gracious gift of life.[132]

The matter of equality of all people of God was of primary importance to Jesus. He prayed that all Christians irrespective of nationality, sex or economic status should be one just as Jesus and the Father are one. With Christ in us and God in Christ, we are brought into complete unity, setting us apart from the world.[133] In Christ Jesus, "There is neither Jew nor Greek, slave nor free, male nor female, for you are all one in Christ Jesus."[134] We are all children of God through faith in Jesus Christ. We have all been united with Christ in baptism and we have therefore become like Christ. Since we now belong to Jesus Christ, we are all true children of Abraham and heirs qualified to inherit the promises, which God made to father Abraham.

In the family, husband and wife should see themselves as children of God who have Christ in them, and are therefore equal. The Christ in the husband is the same Christ in the wife. There is only one Christ. When you do your comparison, you see Christ in

---

[131] (Colossians 3:11).
[132] (1 Peter 3:7)
[133] (John 17:21-23).
[134] (Galatians 3:28).

the spouses and you see parity glaring on your face. The life which both husband and wife live, they live in Christ. Both of them come to God through the same Holy Spirit because of what Christ has done for us. There is no difference. Husband and wife are created in the image of God. Their human dignity must be respected and sustained. Wisdom and commonsense must be applied in our interpretation of spousal equality. A wife must recognize that she is the weaker partner and must respect her husband. If she does not respect her husband she has invested in unhappy marriage. Your husband will love you if you give him respect. In fact, if you wish to have a good marriage, you should be submissive to your husband, such that if he were not a believer, you could win her for Christ. In the same way, husbands have been advised to be considerate as they live with their wives, and treat them with respect as the weaker partner in marriage.

The peculiar and interesting thing about husband and wife is that in marriage a man leaves his father and mother to be united to his wife, and they become one flesh. "So they are no longer two, but one. Therefore what God has joined together let man not separate."[135] There is therefore, no basis for comparison between husband and wife. The two have become one. What are you comparing? They are one and in addition, the fact that they have Jesus affirms spousal equity. "In the Lord, however, woman is not

---

[135] (Matthew 19:5-6).

independent of man, nor man independent of woman. For as woman came from man, so also man is born of woman. But everything is from God."[136] There is no difference between husband and wife. The same Lord Jesus Christ is the Lord of both spouses and he blesses all who call on him. While spouses submit to one another out of reverence for Christ, it is also important to know that "the husband is the head of the wife as Christ is the head of the Church, his body, of which he is the Savior. Now as the Church submits to Christ, so also wives should submit to their husbands in everything."[137]

Let us consider the well-known Christian couple, Priscilla and Aquila.[138] Aquila and Priscilla were Jewish husband and wife who served the Lord with Apostle Paul. In fact, they risked their lives for Paul and for the Church of Christ. They had a Church in their home.[139] They taught the eloquent evangelist Apollos about the Baptism of the Holy Spirit. Aquila and Priscilla were mentioned together seven times in the Holy Bible. In two of the cases, Aquila her husband was mentioned first (i.e. Aquila and Priscilla[140]), while in five cases Priscilla his wife was mentioned first (i.e. Priscilla and Aquila[141]). The more frequent mention of Priscilla than her husband

---

[136] (1 Corinthians 11:11-12).
[137] (Ephesians 5:22-24).
[138] (Acts 18).
[139] (Romans 16:4-5).
[140] Acts 18:2, Romans 16:3
[141] Acts 18:18, 19, 26, 1 Corinthians 16:19, 2 Timothy 4:19

Aquila in the cited passages does not imply that Priscilla was not submissive to her husband. In fact, it meant that she obeyed the commands of God in her relationship with her husband. The spouses, like Paul were tentmakers and they were always together in ministry. There was no basis for comparison between Priscilla and Aquila because there was convincing spousal equity based on respect for human dignity and the understanding by the spouses that Priscilla was the weaker partner. Priscilla was therefore submissive to her husband in everything, while Aquila loved his wife and was not harsh in dealings with her. There was mutual respect for each other out of reverence for Christ. They had a Church in their home and both of them worked to see that everything was going well in the ministry of the Gospel of Jesus. A good example was when they invited Evangelist Apollos to their home and explained to him about baptism with the Holy Ghost. Apollos was teaching about Jesus accurately, but he knew only the baptism of John on which he was speaking boldly about in the synagogue. "When Priscilla and Aquila heard him, they invited him to their home and explained to him the way of God more adequately."[142]

[Each of you in the family should look not only to your own interests, but also to the interest of other family members.]

---

[142] (Acts 18:2-26).

Quest
1. What determines equality in Christ?
2. How does Galatians 3:28, and Ephesians 5:22-33 help to explain spousal equity?
3. Jesus prayed about the unity of all believers and emphasized the need for oneness in Christ. How does the Lord drive home the fact that Christian spouses are heirs of the gracious gift of life? Relate your answer to 1 Peter 3:7. (John 17:20-23).
4. Explain Matthew 23:8 (NLT) and indicate its illumination of the need to sustain human dignity and equal opportunity for all.
5. Discuss Matthew 19:4-6 in relation to spousal mutual submission and respect.
6. Explain the concept of mutuality (Ephesians 5:21) in spousal relations using 1 Corinthians 11:11-12.
7. In what ways may a wife misinterpret spousal equity and run herself into problem, not only with her husband but also with God?
8. How does the marital relationship of Priscilla and Aquila help in a better understanding of mutual submission and respect?
9. If you are married, is there mutual respect and submission in your marriage?

10. How can spousal equity be achieved in a Christian family without ignoring the commandments of God that address marital and family relations?

11. In the concept of spousal equity, how must commonsense and wisdom be used to avoid a dangerous misinterpretation?

Memory Verse: There is neither Jew nor Greek, slave nor free, male nor female, for you are all one in Christ Jesus.[143]

---

[143] (Galatians 3:28).

Study Fifteen

Topic: The Family Altar

Text: The most important contributing factor for sustaining meaningful marital and family relations is the family altar. The presence of a family altar is an indication of honor to God and the desire for marital and family integrity. The reality of your relationship is dependent on your wholehearted dependence on God that is made practicable in the family altar. Joshua said to the Israelites, "If serving the Lord seems undesirable to you, then choose for yourselves this day whom you will serve, whether the gods your forefathers served beyond the River, or the gods of the Amorites, in whose land you are living. But as for me and my household, we will serve the Lord."[144] Joshua, therefore established a family altar. He stood for something and was not ashamed of declaring what he stood for. He stood for serving the true God of heaven. His determination to worship the true God encouraged other Israelites to promise to serve God. If you cannot take a stand for something God, then be sure you will fall for anything.

Ruth told her mother-in-law Naomi, "Don't urge me to leave you or to turn back from you. Where you go I will go, and where you stay I will stay. Your people will be my people, and your God

---

[144] (Joshua 24:15).

my God."[145] Here you see that Ruth stood for something and her stance carried her through to greater heights. On Mount Carmel, Prophet Elijah asked King Ahab and the people of Israel, "How long will you waver between two opinions? If the Lord is God, follow him; but if Baal is God, follow him."[146] Ahab and his subjects worshipped Baal and paid lip service to the true God of heaven. Baal could not send fire because it is powerless. The God of Elijah is the true God of heaven. He sent fire that consumed the sacrifice of Elijah. If you do not stand for God in your family, both your marriage and family will not endure. The marriage and family of King Ahab and her wife Jezebel met a disastrous end because they turned their back against the true God of heaven.

God blessed the family of the Recabites because they stood for something that was right and honorable. "Jonadab the son of Recab ordered his sons not to drink wine and this command has been kept. To this day they do not drink wine because they obey their forefather's command."[147] Then Jeremiah said, to the family of the Recabites, "This is what the Lord Almighty, the God of Israel says: 'You have obeyed the command of your forefather, Jonadab and have followed all his instructions and have done everything he ordered. Therefore, this is what the Lord Almighty, the God of Israel says: 'Jonadab son of Recab will never fail to have a man to

---

[145] (Ruth 1:16).
[146] (1 Kings 18:21).

serve me."[148] The strong family altar of the Recabites can be compared to the family altar in Obed-Edom's home. Obed-Edom's family had housed the Ark of Covenant of the Lord for three months, and the Lord blessed his household and everything they had.[149] Everyone, including David was afraid of keeping the Ark of Covenant at this time because of the death of Uzzah after he had irreverently touched the stumbling Ark. The courage of Obed-Edom and his family was unprecedented at this terrifying moment. Some people would not host a Christian meeting because participants would mess up their floor carpet creating work and causing an unbudgeted expenditure.

Time has come when families should begin to realize that the way to go is to serve the Living God, sustaining worship by the family altar. "Josiah removed all the detestable idols from all the territory belonging to the Israelites, and he had all who were present in Israel serve the Lord their God. As long as he lived, they did not fail to follow the Lord, the God of their fathers."[150] Elkanah also had a family altar in his home. He also connected well with the temple in Jerusalem. Elkanah and his family went to the Temple of God in Jerusalem every year to make sacrifices and fulfill his vow to God.[151] There was a family altar in the home of Joseph of Nazareth and the

---

[147] (Jeremiah 35:14).
[148] (Jeremiah 35:18-19).
[149] (1 Chronicles 13:14).
[150] (2 Chronicles 34:33).

Virgin Mary. They also connected well with the Temple of God in Jerusalem.[152] The family altar requires that family members conduct themselves in a way that brings honor to God and respect for the family. A spouse does not go into a disagreement with someone outside the family just because his/her spouse has disagreed with that person. Don't prejudge something because your spouse is involved. You need to ask questions, investigate and probe the situation prayerfully before you can take a stand. Your stance must be sensible, such that the possibility of achieving a peaceful settlement is not ruined by any precipitate action. You must not support any questionable actions of members of your family without thoroughly examining the basis for their action. You could embarrass yourself if you are not careful, and in doing so you could block avenues for redress. Always stand for the truth and seek peace in love with all your might. If you condone evil in your family, that evil may haunt you in future.

[Each of you in the family should look not only to your own interests, but also to the interest of other family members.]

---

[151] (1 Samuel 1:21).
[152] (Luke 2:41-52).

Quest

1. What do you mean by a family altar?
2. How can a family altar represent one of the most important assets of marriage and family?
3. Explain how Joshua's declaration in Joshua 24:15 point to the family altar?
4. What is the importance of standing for what is right?
5. How does Ruth demonstrate the type of sincere love that family altar can generate?
6. Why did God bless the Recabites?
7. Relate the hosting of Christian ministry events in your home to Obed-Edom's housing of the Ark of Covenant?
8. How do Elkanah and Joseph of Nazareth reveal the relationship between the family altar and the Church?
9. Discuss the dangers of going into a quarrel with somebody outside your family just because your spouse or child is quarrelling with that person?
10. How may family altar increase the integrity of members of your family?

Memory Verse: But if serving the Lord seems undesirable to you, then choose for yourselves this day whom you will serve, whether the gods your forefathers served beyond the River, or the gods of the

Amorites, in whose land you are living. But as for me and my household, we will serve the Lord.[153]

---

[153] (Joshua 24:15).

Study Sixteen

Topic: Chauvinistic Tendencies

Text: One of the most disruptive factors against family peace and endurance is the chauvinistic attitude of some husbands against their wives. Chauvinistic treatment of women by men has generated wife-battering, and men cheating (infidelity) on their wives with reckless abandon. The man may cheat and go scot-free, but when his wife cheats it becomes an abomination. Yes, it is an abomination for a wife to cheat on her husband and it is also equally an abomination for the husband to cheat on his wife. Husbands are supposed to be considerate as they live with their wives, and treat them with respect as the weaker partner. Men should therefore be considerate and not cheat on their wives. To cheat on your wife is a humiliation and disrespect for her human dignity. You are sort of asking "what can she do?" Remember, that God will come to her defense! Therefore be careful, and do not break the heart of your wife. None of you should cheat on the other.

The concept of oneness of husband and wife is a divine construct and not just a matter for human manipulation. The teachers of the Law and the Pharisees brought a woman caught in adultery and reported her to Jesus saying, "Teacher, this woman was caught in adultery. In the Law, Moses commanded us to stone such women. Now what do you say?"[154] Jesus replied them, "If any one of you is without sin, let him be the first to throw a stone at her." None of them cast a stone on the woman. In fact, they all went away embarrassed because they were not better than the woman caught in adultery. They did not even bring forward to Jesus the man who committed adultery with the woman. The action of the chauvinistic Jewish people was very unfair. Jesus forgave the woman and told her not to live a life of sin any more.

Many of the early apostles still had elements of the Mosaic chauvinistic tendencies. The understanding was that they were operating in a traditional chauvinistic society. The integration of women had to be a gradual process if that society was to be persuaded to embrace the Gospel of Jesus. It was not only the integration of women in ministry that required patience, but also the total rejection of Mosaic Law was delayed. For instance, Apostle Paul who preached strongly against circumcision of the flesh circumcised Timothy because of his fear of the Jews.[155] Paul knew that Priscilla and Aquila invited the eloquent preacher Apollos, to their home and explained to him the way of God more adequately.[156] It was the same Apostle Paul who told Timothy, "A woman should learn in quietness and full submission. I do not permit a woman to

---

[154] (John 8:4-5).
[155] (Acts 16:3).
[156] (Acts 18:26).

teach or to have authority over a man; she must be silent."[157] Timothy was Greek. He was appointed to pastor a predominantly Jewish congregation. Timothy had a sincere faith, which first lived in his grandmother Lois and in his mother Eunice.[158] With this background Timothy would give women equal freedom with men in all activities of the Church. Paul perceived that if Timothy did so he would run into problems with such a predominantly Jewish congregation.

Apostle Paul needed to convince Timothy to agree to suppress women activities in his congregation. He said, "For Adam was formed first, then Eve. And Adam was not the one deceived; it was the woman who was deceived and became a sinner. But women will be saved through childbearing – if they continue in faith, love and holiness with propriety."[159] Paul was citing the curse placed on the woman during the fall of man.[160] The curse was not divinely intended. It was caused by sin. Jesus Christ removed the curse with the shedding of his blood. "Christ redeemed us from the curse by becoming a curse for us, for it is written: "Cursed is everyone who is hung on a tree."[161] Even before his death, Jesus preemptively invoked the power of the blood when she forgave the woman caught

---

[157] (1 Timothy 2: 11).
[158] (2 Timothy 1:5).
[159] (1 Timothy 2:13-15).
[160] (Genesis 3:16).
[161] (Galatians 3:13).

in adultery. Jesus completely erased all discriminatory practices against women.

Jesus saw in women the essential ingredient required for the growth of the Kingdom of God. He delivered them from male chauvinism and placed women in a position of prominence in the Gospel. The honor which Jesus has given to women was very well illuminated during his ministry here on earth. At his resurrection he showed himself first to a woman, Mary Magdalene. The same woman was the first to announce the Good News to the male Apostles and the rest of the world, "I have seen the Lord."[162] It will be noted that during one of the visits to the tomb by Mary Magdalene and other women, they were met by an angel who said to them, "Do not be afraid, for I know that you are looking for Jesus, who was crucified. He is not here; he has risen, just as he said. Come and see where he lay. Then go quickly and tell his disciples: 'He has risen from the dead and is going ahead of you into Galilee. There you will see him."[163]

If the angel told the women to go and tell the male disciples of Jesus, that Christ had risen from death, it is inconceivable that Paul would order women to be silent about the Gospel and even tell them not to teach in the presence of men. Paul's recommendation to Timothy was only to address the situation in the predominantly

---

[162] (John 20:18).
[163] (Matthew 28:5-8).

Jewish congregation in which Timothy was pastor. It has earlier been noted that Paul himself circumcised Timothy in order to escape danger from the Jews. To prove that Paul's statements should not be taken out of context, Paul said, "Mark my words! I, Paul, tell you that if you let yourself be circumcised, Christ will be of no value to you at all."[164] It will be noted that Paul was in ministry and he was confronted with various situations that required contextualized instructions. His statements should not be taken out of context. For instance, the conclusion of all he said about circumcision and which is universally applicable in the Kingdom of God is, "For in Christ Jesus neither circumcision nor uncircumcision has any value. The only thing that counts is faith expressing itself through love."[165] Similarly, what Paul said about women that is universally applicable in the Kingdom of God is, "There is neither Jew nor Greek, slave nor free, male nor female, for you are all one in Christ Jesus."[166] Jesus himself said, "All of you are on the same level as brothers and sisters."[167] This means that males and females should be given equal opportunity to apply their talents for the benefit of the Gospel of Christ. Both sexes are running the race for eternal life and eternal life is the same for all.

---

[164] (Galatians 5:2).
[165] (Galatians 5:6, 6:15).
[166] (Galatians 3:28).
[167] (Matthew 23:8b NLT).

It will be noted that it was the command of Paul and not that of God that women should learn in quietness and full submission.[168] Paul's statement was contextual - relating to the situation at hand in the congregation in which Timothy served as pastor. Apostle Paul taught, "Submit to one another out of reverence for Christ."[169] He also said, "For this reason a man will leave his father and mother and be united to his wife, and the two will become one flesh." 'This is a profound mystery – but I am talking about Christ and the Church. However, each one of you also must love his wife as he loves himself, and the wife must respect her husband.'[170] In order to understand where Saint Paul was coming from in his various contextual statements, he concluded as follows, "In the Lord, however, woman is not independent of man, nor is man independent of woman. For as woman came from man, so also man is born of woman. But everything is from God."[171]

Men should stop restricting women from doing the work of God. The harvest is plenty, but the laborers are few. We need women in all areas of ministry. Without their input, our Churches will be no Churches, and our homes will be no homes. Many women are very talented and are doing excellently well in the ministry of the Gospel. It is unfortunate that from the outset, the Gospel has been

---

[168] (1 Timothy 2:12).
[169] (Ephesians 5:21).
[170] (Ephesians 5:31-33).
[171] (1 Corinthians 11:11-12).

negatively affected by male chauvinism and Mosaic practices. However, in Christ things have been put right. It is now time to wriggle out of Pharisaic and chauvinistic practices, and allow the Holy Spirit to guide us into what is obtainable in Christ Jesus. We can no longer circumcise Timothy or suppress women in order to be safe while preaching the Gospel. We are now completely entrenched in the Kingdom of God, and we no longer have to fear any one as we go about preaching the Good News about Jesus.

Life in the family is scripturally similar to life in the Church. It is therefore necessary for members of the family to understand that in marriage, the husband is the head of the wife as Christ is the head of the Church, his body, of which he is the Savior. The husband should also protect her wife from extraneous factors that could threaten her well-being. The Church submits to Christ, so also wives should submit to their husbands in everything,[172] while children should obey their parents just as Church members obey the Lord.[173]

[Each of you in the family should look not only to your own interests, but also to the interest of other family members.]

---

[172] (Ephesians 5:23-24)
[173] (Ephesians 6:1)

Quest

1. Explain male chauvinism.
2. The woman caught in adultery was brought to Jesus for condemnation. Discuss Jesus' handling of the matter. (John 8:1-11).
3. Apostle Paul circumcised Timothy (Acts 16:3) and yet he said, "Mark my words! I, Paul, tell you that if you let yourself be circumcised, Christ will be of no value to you at all." (Galatians 5:2). Could this be explained as hypocrisy?
4. Apostle Paul knows that women at the tomb were sent by the angel of God to tell the male disciples of Jesus that Christ had risen from death. He also knows that in Christ males and females are at the same level. Paul told Timothy that women should learn in quietness and are not permitted by him to teach. Why should Paul not be taken out of context? (Note that it was Paul's command and not the Lord's).
5. Illuminate the contribution of Mosaic Law to male chauvinism.
6. What response will you give to male chauvinists who say that the place of the woman is only in the home?
7. People who prevent women from using their talents in the ministry of the Gospel of Christ, are reducing the workforce in ministry. Discuss.

8. What contribution does Paul make to the concept of spousal equity in his statement of Galatians 3:28.

9. How may wife-battering be connected to male chauvinism?

10. Do you think that women have now been given complete freedom in all denominations to serve the Lord to their full potential?

11. What is the situation in your Church on the subject of allowing women full freedom to minister?

Memory Verse: Jesus said, if any one of you is without sin, let him be the first to throw a stone at her.[174]

---

[174] (John 8:7b).

Study Seventeen

Topic: Keeping the Faith

Text: In marriage and family, changes occur, sometimes so suddenly that one may not be prepared for them. When changes occur, adjustments will need to be made in the family to keep things going. When one goes into marriage, the thoughts of painful changes are often regarded as an anathema. However, certain changes are natural processes that one cannot do anything about. One would not need to begin early in marriage to get worried about future changes in the status quo. Such thoughts may imply negative thinking. The Christian hope is that it will be all right in the Lord, "being confident of this, that he who began a good work in you will carry it on to completion until the day of Christ."[175] To have such hope, ones marital and family relationships must be Christ-centered and supported with the spiritual disciplines of prayer, Bible studies, fellowship, discipleship etc.

A Christian needs a job because we are encouraged to keep away from people who claim to be Christians but are idle. Idle people are busybodies who can get themselves into trouble very easily. We are commanded in the Lord Jesus Christ to earn the bread we eat. "Whoever does not work should not eat."[176] Therefore,

---

[175] (Philippians 1:6).
[176] (2 Thessalonians 3:10 NLT).

"make it your ambition to lead a quiet life, to mind your business and to work with your hands, just as we told you, so that your daily life may win the respect of outsiders and so that you will not be dependent on any body."[177] Invest your talent so that you will have something in the bank to fall back to when the need arises. What do you have in your hand? Use it and keep the faith, no matter what. If you are a person that has lived the prodigal type of life, come to your senses and return to the Lord. However, if you have done everything excellently, but yet nemesis has caught up with you, and now you no longer wish to be called Naomi, but Mara (bitterness), escape from the land of famine and the Lord will wipe the tears in your eyes.[178]

The widow of a well-known prophet was beleaguered by the creditors of her late husband. She remained in faith after the death of her husband. She went to the man of God, Prophet Elisha to seek help. This means that she cast her cares on the Lord. The creditors of her husband were determined to take her two sons to serve them as slaves. The widow said to Prophet Elisha, "Your servant has nothing in the house except a little oil."[179] It was a bold step that paid off. Prophet Elisha said to her, "Go around and ask all your neighbors for empty jars. Don't ask for just a few. Then go inside and shut the door behind you and your sons. Pour oil into all the

---

[177] (1 Thessalonians 4:11-12).
[178] (Ruth 1:20-22).
[179] (2 Kings 4:2).

jars, and as each is filled, put it to one side."[180] The widow and her children did what the man of God told them. She sold the oil and paid off her family debts. They also lived with what was left after the debts were paid.

Although the husband of this woman had departed to be with the Lord, she remained faithful to her responsibilities in her family. Above all, she remained fully connected to God. She sought help from a person of God and not from elsewhere. Her humility can also be seen in the respect she had for the man of God. She said, "Your servant has nothing in the house at all except a little oil." She also obeyed the instructions of the man of God. Obedience to the word of God is an important aspect of righteousness. A widow should not fall out of faith, otherwise she would create the impression that her faith was originally dependent on her husband. Widows and widowers must sustain their faith and be role models in the Lord for their children.

[Each of you in the family should look not only to your own interests, but also to the interest of other family members.]

---

[180] (2 Kings 4:3-4).

Quest

1. What changes could be destabilizing to marriage and family relationships?
2. Should spouses and members of their family worry themselves over changes that have not yet occurred?
3. What should be the Christian hope when one begins to think about changes in the status quo?
4. How may gainful employment and investments be helpful preparation for any unexpected changes?
5. How may spouses sustain their faith in the event of changes taking place in the family?
6. The widow in the text was confronted with a very difficult situation when a painful change occurred. Discuss her handing of the matter.
7. It does not appear that her husband left any wealth. In fact, he left a lot of debt. Explore the faithfulness of her wife to their marriage and family.
8. What factors show that she was a person of God?
9. What impression does a widow or widower create when he/she falls out of faith?

Memory Verse: The widow said to Prophet Elisha, "Your servant has nothing in the house except a little oil."[181]

---

[181] (2 Kings 4:2).

Study Eighteen

Topic: Role of a Father

Text: This study will present the father as a husband with one wife and child/children. He is the overseer of his family. For instance, Job had seven sons and three daughters. His sons used to take turns holding feasts, probably during their respective birthdays in their homes. When a period of feasting is completed, Job would purify his children and make sacrifices to God for each child on the grounds that "Perhaps my children have sinned and cursed God in their hearts."[182] The priest Eli warned his disobedient children who were sleeping with women who came to worship God in the Temple, "Why do you do such things? I hear from all the people about these wicked deeds of yours. No, my sons; it is not a good report that I hear spreading among the Lord's people. If a man sins against another man, God may mediate for him; but if a man sins against the Lord, who will intercede for him?"[183] Simeon and Levi had killed all the men of a Hivite city because their sister Dinah was defiled by Shechem, Jacob said to his sons Simeon and Levi, "You have brought trouble on me by making me a stench to the Canaanites and

---

[182] (Job 1:5).
[183] (1 Samuel 2:23-25).

Perizzites, the people living in this land. We are few in number, I and my household will be destroyed."[184]

A father should therefore be an overseer in his family. He should be above reproach, temperate, self-controlled, respectable, hospitable, able to teach his children, not given to drunkenness, not violent but gentle, and not quarrelsome. He must manage his own family well and see that his children obey him with proper respect. A father is supposed to be a role model for his children. It has been indicated that he should be above reproach. This means that he should not do anything that will bring disgrace or shame not only to him but also to his family. People talk about a good or a bad family. The type of family - whether good or bad, is largely dependent on the role of the father. He must live by good example and set the pace for trustworthy actions. Some fathers fall short a lot. This should not be the case. A father must be a man of one and only one wife. He should not sleep with another woman, otherwise he would break the heart of his wife and hurt his children. He must not keep more than one home, and that single home must be with his wife and children.

A father must be temperate. He should show moderation in action, exercising restraint and not given to overdriven anger. He should be compassionately strict, ensuring that there is wisdom in his strictness. Anger must not overtake moderation and result in senseless actions, such as wife or child battering. Any such actions

---

[184] (Genesis 34:30).

are an indication that Satan is in control. Wife battering is also an indication that the concept of unity of flesh in marriage is abrogated. Wife battering is a crazy action. The perpetrating husband becomes a threat to the life of his wife who cannot be blamed for taking actions like elopement to escape death. A battering father is a violent person characterized by lack of self-control. He fails to understand that husbands ought to love their wives as their own bodies. He who loves his wife loves himself, while he who hates his wife hates himself.[185] A battering father is manipulated by satanic hate and he is a dangerous person to do business with. He seeks control through inhuman dominance. When he becomes angry, his anger could cause senseless destruction of family property including what he has sweated to provide for his family. A father who is neither temperate nor has self-control can be a quarrelsome person who would pick quarrel easily with his wife and children. A father who does not love his wife sincerely is operating in the domain of the devil. He should love his wife and ensure that her concerns are taken seriously. He should give sufficient quality time to his wife because his wife is his best friend. If he does not give his wife quality time and listen to her, he could stimulate her to begin looking for someone who would lend her listening ear and tell her what she would like to hear. He should not let anyone or anything disconnect him from his wife.

---

[185] (Ephesians 5:28, 33).

A father should be a role model. The only realistic way of achieving this status is for his life to be Christ-like. A father should be the priest of his home who does those things that will generate peace and harmony in his home. A father should be responsible for the good functioning of his family, just as Christ is responsible to the Church, which he is the head. The father is a man of integrity who is sincere in his dealings and also worthy of respect. One could not be a good father if he does not know the word of God. He should also ensure that members of his family know and apply the word of God in their various activities. The father ought to be a strong member of his local Church, and also goes to Church on a regular basis with all members of his family. The family altar should be sustained through the integrity and faithfulness of the father. A father should be gainfully employed in order to command the respect not only of his household, but also of outsiders. His paying job should provide the needs of his family. He must also encourage other members of his family to be hardworking in all areas of life. Care must be taken by a father to ensure that only honest gains are brought into the family.

In conclusion, a father is a husband who loves his wife just as Christ loved the Church and gave himself up for her to make her holy, cleansing her by the washing with water through the word of God and to present her to himself as a radiant Church, without a stain or wrinkle or any other blemish, but holy and blameless. In the same way a father ought to love his wife as his own body. He should be considerate and treat his wife with respect as a biologically weaker partner and as heirs to the kingdom of God.[186] A father should love his wife and should not be harsh with her. He should not embitter his children or they will become discouraged.[187] A father should not exasperate his children; instead he should bring them up in the training and instruction of the Lord.[188] A father should know that he is the pride of his children. He is the light through which the public recognizes those children as quality persons. A father must not minimize this fact through irresponsibility.

[Each of you in the family should look not only to your own interests, but also to the interest of other family members.]

Quest

1. What are the roles of an overseer?
2. In what instances did the following fathers play the role of overseer in their homes: Job, Eli, and Jacob?
3. In what ways has your spouse/father served your family as an overseer?
4. According to the text, what are the qualifications of a father?
5. Can a battering father be regarded as a loving father?

---

[186] (1 Peter 3:7).
[187] (Colossians 3:19, 21).
[188] (Ephesians 6:4).

6. Suggest what a woman who is consistently battered by a husband should do to prevent her husband from battering her.
7. Give examples of trustworthy actions.
8. How dangerous can a battering father be to members of his family?
9. How may self-control be the most important quality of a father?
10. What is the importance of a paying job to a father?
11. Suggest the importance of a father giving quality time to his wife and children.
12. Compare the role of the father as husband of his wife with the role of Jesus as head of his Church.
13. An absentee father is not a father. Discuss.

Memory Verse: Husbands, in the same way be considerate as you live with your wives, and treat them with respect as the weaker partner and as heirs with you of the gracious gift of life, so that nothing will hinder your prayers.[189]

---

[189] (1 Peter 3:7).

Study Nineteen

Topic: Role of Mother

Text: A mother is the wife of a father in a home. She is a symbol of peace and harmony and she also represents care and nurturance. A mother is synonymous with a home. For a mother to be a true mother she is to be God-fearing. Hannah had gone to the Temple of God to pray to God for a child. She promised that if God gave her a son, she would give him back to God. The Lord answered her prayers and gave her a son. She brought her son Samuel to Eli the priest and said to him, "As surely as you live, my lord I am the woman who stood here beside you praying to the Lord. I prayed for this child and the Lord has granted me what I asked of him. So now I give him to the Lord. For his whole life he will be given over to the Lord."[190] A mother is a good and gentle teacher of her children. Timothy was taught the word of God by his mother and grandmother. Paul reminded Timothy, "I have been reminded of the sincere faith, which first lived in your grandmother Lois and in your mother Eunice and, I am persuaded, now lives in you also. For this reason I remind you to fan into flame the gift of God, which is in you through the laying on of my hands."[191] The mother of King Lemuel of Massa taught him:

---

[190] (1 Samuel 1:26-28).
[191] (2 Timothy 1:5-6).

"O my son, O son of my womb, O son of my vows, do not spend your strength on women, your vigor on those who ruin kings.

It is not for kings, O Lemuel – not for kings to drink wine, not for rulers to crave beer, lest they drink and forget what the law decrees, and deprive all the oppressed of their rights. Give beer to those who are perishing, wine to those who are in anguish; let them drink and forget their poverty and remember their misery no more.

Speak up for those who cannot speak for themselves, for the rights of all who are destitute. Speak up and judge fairly; defend the rights of the poor and needy."[192]

A mother has a very good understanding of her children. At a wedding ceremony in Cana in Galilee, the mother of Jesus said to him, "They have no more wine." And she turned to the wine servers and advised them, "Do whatever he tells you."[193] The servants complied with the instructions and Jesus miraculously converted water into the best wine ever. A mother is very caring and concerned about the welfare and safety of her children. Joseph's family had

---

[192] (Proverbs 31:1-9).
[193] (John 2:3, 5).

gone to worship at the Temple in Jerusalem. After the ceremony, Joseph and his wife Mary the mother of Jesus could not see their son Jesus. After three days, they found him in the Temple courts, sitting among the teachers, listening to them and asking them questions. Everyone who heard Jesus was amazed at his great understanding and exact answers he gave to difficult questions. When his parents saw him with the teachers of the law, they were astonished. Jesus' mother said to him, "Son, why have you treated us like this? Your father and I have been anxiously searching for you." Jesus replied his parents with the question, "Why were you searching for me. Didn't you know I had to be in my Father's house?"[194]

A mother is a wife who loves her husband and respects him. She is to submit to her husband in everything just as the Church submits to Christ.[195] Wives who are submissive to their husbands become agents of the gospel of Christ. "Wives, in the same way be submissive to your husbands so that, if any of them do not believe the word, they may be won over without words by the behavior of their wives, when they see the purity and reverence of your lives."[196] The beauty of a wife should not come from outward adornment, such as braided hair and the wearing of gold jewelry and fine clothes. "Charm is deceptive, and beauty is fleeting; but a woman who fears

---

[194] (Luke 2:48-49).
[195] (Ephesians 5:24, 33, Colossians 3:18).
[196] (1 Peter 3:1-2).

the Lord is to be praised."[197] The beauty of a wife/mother should be that of the inner person characterized by the unfading beauty of a gentle and quiet spirit. Sarah the wife of Abraham was submissive to her husband and even called him master. Holy women of the past like Sarah made themselves beautiful by putting their trust and hope in God. The Virgin Mary and Hannah, cited earlier are among such holy God-fearing women. Modern women should take their bearing from the good lives lived by such great women who were both wives and mothers. A wife should stimulate respect for her husband through her good behavior. In fact, her husband and children should have full confidence in her. She brings good to her husband, not harm all the days of her life. She should not involve herself in blackmailing her husband before his children and outsiders for selfish ends. Infidelity should not even be mentioned in her life as a wife. It is infidelity that would destroy her person and her relationship, not only with her husband, but also with her children. Infidelity will make her lose her credibility as a wife because it messes her up.

A wife should be hardworking and be able to generate extra resources for meeting the needs of her family. "She considers a field and buys it; out of her earnings she plants a vineyard. She sets about her work vigorously; her arms are strong for her tasks. She sees that her trading is profitable, and her lamp does not go out at night."[198]

---

[197] (Proverbs 31:30).
[198] (Proverbs 31:16-17).

An idle wife/mother could be a busybody and the source of family problems. Rebekah provided good food for her husband Isaac and her children, Esau and Jacob. She knew the type of food her husband liked so she prepared it and gave to Jacob to present to his father Isaac. He enjoyed the food and blessed Jacob even before the arrival of Esau.[199] A wife/mother should provide food for her family. She should be concerned about the welfare of all members of her family. She must always be fired up about things of God and stimulate all members of her family to be effectively involved in the family altar and in the local Church. Therefore, her life of purity cannot here be overemphasized.

[Each of you in the family should look not only to your own interests, but also to the interest of other family members.]

Quest

1. "A mother is synonymous with a home." Discuss.
2. How did Hannah show that she was God-fearing?
3. What examples are given in the text to show that mothers are good teachers?
4. How did the mother of King Lemuel reveal that caring for the poor is important?

---

[199] (Genesis 27:25-30).

5. If the Virgin Mary knew that her son Jesus could miraculously provide wine at the wedding in Cana, was it Jesus' first miracle?
6. Discuss the broader view of the Virgin Mary's advice, "Do whatever he tells you."
7. Discuss the impression about Mary the mother of Jesus in relation to his husband and son from her statement, "Son, why have you treated us like this? Your father and I have been anxiously searching for you."
8. Discuss spiritual importance of a wife's submission to her husband?
9. How may the submission of a wife to her husband guarantee mutual submission of husband and wife?
10. According Christian principles, where does the beauty of a wife come from?
11. How does the credibility of a wife/mother depend on her being God-fearing?
12. Discuss how wife infidelity minimizes her role in the family?

Memory Verse: Charm is deceptive, and beauty is fleeting; but a woman who fears the Lord is to be praised.[200]

---

[200] (Proverbs 31:30).

Study Twenty

Topic: Factors in Marriage and Family

Discipline

It is important to know that we all fall short from time to time. It is therefore necessary to have a deterrent as a means helping us out. This indispensable deterrent is discipline. In fact, a person who ignores discipline despises himself/herself, but whoever heeds correction gains understanding.[201] God himself disciplines us to put us right because we are his children. You should count yourself blessed when the Lord disciplines you.[202] People sometimes stray very far away from God in their acts of sin. God may seek our attention through discipline in order that we may come to our senses like the prodigal son.[203] "Endure hardship as discipline; God is treating you as his sons. For what son is not disciplined by his father? If you are not disciplined (and everyone undergoes discipline), then you are illegitimate children and not true sons."[204] In the family, therefore, no person should be above discipline. If you refuse discipline from members of the family, God may seek your attention with more difficult discipline. When family members turn their backs

---

[201] (Proverbs 15:32).
[202] (Psalm 94:12).
[203] (Luke 15:17).
[204] (Hebrews 12:7-12).

against God, they run themselves into very serious problems. The hardship they cause themselves may simply be a divine attempt to seek their attention. This would make them seek the will of God for their family. The Family of King Ahab and Jezebel turned their backs against God and served Baal instead. They were so wicked that they killed Naboth and took his land.[205] They perished with their seventy children almost within a few days.[206] If you do not want anyone to discipline you, then you should discipline yourself by exercising self-control in the fear of the Lord. Otherwise you will die for lack of discipline, led astray by your own great folly.[207] "But if we judge ourselves, we would not come under judgment. When we are judged by the Lord, we are being disciplined so that we will not be condemned with the world."[208] Your family will not judge you when you discipline yourself. Family members discipline one another as a demonstration of love. They do not want any family member to become a reproach and cause harm to any member. God himself says, "Those whom I love I rebuke and discipline. So be earnest and repent. Here I am! I stand at the door and knock. If anyone hears my voice and opens the door, I will come in and eat with him, and he

---

[205] (1 Kings 21).
[206] (2 Kings 10:1-8).
[207] (Proverbs 5:23).
[208] (1 Corinthians 11:31-32).

with me."[209] Members of your family will not even eat with you if you fail to accept discipline and turn from your evil ways.

Children should be appropriately disciplined by their parents. Discipline, your child, for in that there is hope; do not be a willing party to his death.[210] If you do not begin early to discipline your child, you might not be able to do it effectively later. Your undisciplined child may bring pain and disgrace to your family. In fact, if you do not discipline your child, he/she could be the cause of death in your family. Undisciplined children are causing havoc nowadays in the society. The situation is reaching such an alarming proportion that guns are being used indiscriminately at home and outside the home by undisciplined children. "Do not withhold discipline from a child; if you punish him with the rod, he will not die. Punish him with the rod and save his soul from death."[211] Any disciplinary measure you adopt should be strict and of course reasonable, making sure that the aim of discipline is not to cause physical injury but to produce a deterrent against deviance. If you are unable to create this deterrent, the child will create the deterrent in you when both of you may perish. A youth was raining heavy blows with clenched fists on his mother as he was yelling on his "mom you cannot do me anything." He was sitting on the passenger seat while his mother was holding the steering wheel. People feared for that

---

[209] (Revelation 3:19-20).
[210] (Proverbs 19:18).
[211] (Proverbs 13-14).

woman's life as it was uncertain what was going to happen to her when they reached home.

Finances

Every family must aspire to a good financial standing in order to be able to provide the needs of members. Living wage of members will contribute to good finances for the family. Where possible, members should be gainfully employed. No bad habits that could waste family funds should be allowed. Members should spend money for common good, not for selfish motives. There should therefore be accountability in financial dealings. Husband's income becomes wife's income and vice versa. Since husband and wife are one flesh, they own things together. There should be no love of money in the family because the love of money is the root of all evils. Some spouses marry because of the wealth which they see in the other spouse and not because of love. There have been cases in which a spouse murders his/her partner in order to acquire his/her wealth. Therefore, be careful when you wish to get married. Some people come for your wealth and not for marriage. You need divine guidance if you wish to get a true spouse.

When you get married to the person who loves you for marriage and not for your wealth, you will then organize your finances in a way that will honor God and provide the needs of your family. Such organization of your finances may involve mutual agreement of spouses in all areas. Gambling and unreasonable use of credit cards should be avoided. Buy only what you need. Some people claim to love shopping, and end up increasing credit card debt. If you do not have the money for your shopping zeal then you should control that zeal. Never involve yourself in debt without the knowledge of your spouse. Financial accountability is helpful to ensure cordial family relations. If this accountability is not there, family funds could go into sinful acts such as infidelity. A point must be reached where spousal integrity must be guaranteed so that spouses would have implicit confidence in one another. Children should be made to realize that they should not spend their parent's money with reckless abandon. They need guidance in financial matters. If parents fail to guide them, they would not focus on those things that would prepare them for a good future.

Church

The Church is a very important contributor to family stability and endurance. The family should be strongly connected to the Church. Through a sound knowledge of the word of God, family members become God-fearing. This is the only way trust can be established among family members. Members of the family should always seek spiritual growth in the Lord and involve themselves in Church ministries. They should pay their tithes to the Church and support the Lord's work generously. The family altar is an aspect of

Christian growth that must be embraced by your family. Family members should hold morning and evening worship at home making intercessions to God for family members and other people. If your family loves the Lord, you will be blessed in all areas of life, just the way the family of Obed-Edom was blessed because they housed the Ark of Covenant for three months. Families need to house the Ark of Covenant of the Lord as Obed-Edom and his family. When Joshua said, "But as for me and my household, we will serve the Lord," his family was metaphorically housing the Ark of Covenant of the Lord. Your family altar is a housing of the Ark of Covenant. Obed-Edom was involved with his household, the way Joshua and his household were involved in honoring God. In your family, care must be taken to ensure that all members join in honoring the Lord. Families who have a Church in their homes are also housing the Ark of Covenant. When your family agrees to host a Christian meeting, you are housing the Ark of Covenant and you will be blessed in the same way as Obed-Edom and his family.[212]

[Each of you in the family should look not only to your own interests, but also to the interest of other family members.]

---

[212] (1 Chronicles 13:14).

Quest

1. Discuss the importance of discipline in a family.
2. How may God seek the attention of a family or any of its members?
3. A family member who disciplines himself/herself does not need further discipline. Discuss.
4. What is the contribution of Revelation 3:19-20 to family discipline?
5. "Do not withhold discipline from a child; if you punish him with the rod, he will not die. Punish him with the rod and save his soul from death." (Proverbs 13-14). Discuss.
6. What could prompt the youth cited in the text to make her mother a punching bag?
7. Discuss the importance of good financial management in a family?
8. What practices could jeopardize family finances?
9. Explain the need for accountability in financial matters in a family?
10. What is the importance of a meaningful connection of the family to the Church?
11. How does Obed-Edom's housing of the Ark of Covenant apply to the various ways in which your family can honor God?

Memory Verse: Discipline your son, and he will give you peace; he will bring delight to your soul.[213]

---

[213] (Proverbs 29:17).

Printed in the United States
45185LVS00002B/808-825